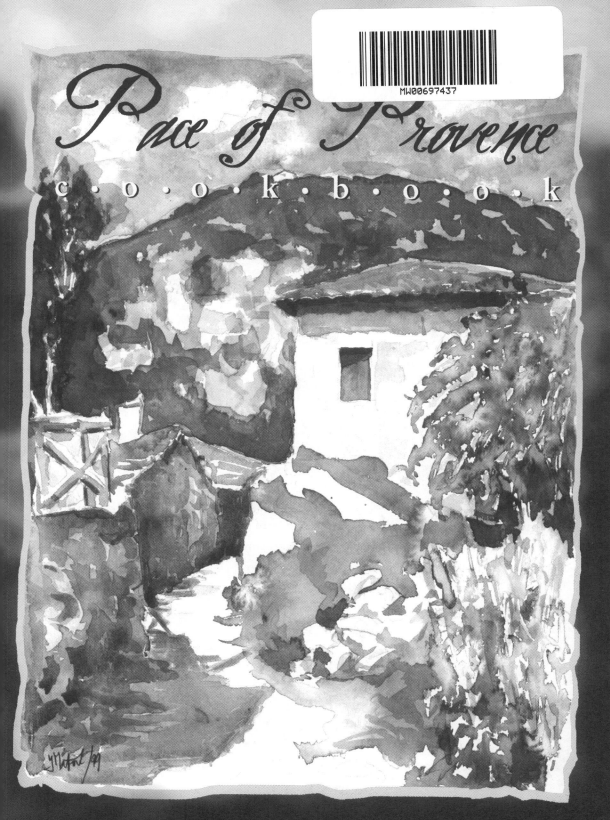

Pace of Provence

c · o · o · k · b · o · o · k

Yolande Matoré Hoisington

Elfin Cove Press
1481 130th Avenue NE
Bellevue, WA 98005
www.elfincovepress.com

Project manager: Bernie Kuntz
Cover Design: Jason Pope
Text Design: Amy Peloff
Illustrations: Yolande Matoré Hoisington

ISBN 0-944958-31-1 soft cover

Printed in the United States of America
1 3 5 7 9 10 8 6 4 2

To Leta
I hope you will like this book
Bon Appetit and good luck!
Yolande

To my grandfather, Emile Matoré, and father, Georges Matoré, both artists and cooks. They encouraged me to continue the tradition of "l'art de vivre" and gave me the desire to write this book. Pace of Provence *is a very personal book, for in it, I share the recipes I cook on a daily basis and the way I deal with food in my life. I am a French woman living in America. Though I have many demands on my time, I make space in each day to cook. Along with cooking, art is a passion for me. It seems natural to include my paintings in a book about how I live. I hope my illustrations help you better understand the way I feel about food and the joy I derive from cooking.*

Contents

Recipe List

The French Way to Healthy Living

Eating Healthy and Feeling Well!

In America, we hear a lot of talk about diet and its relation to health and disease prevention. We all agree a healthy diet and a fulfilling lifestyle are essential. Everyone cares about the fat content of food and choosing ingredients that keep the cholesterol level down. Some of us are even ready to pay more for organic foods, and many are vegetarians. While people constantly worry and talk about dieting, many are over-weight. We often have large kitchens and huge refrigerators but little healthy food in them. There is a lot of talk about "family values", but few families eat meals together, many people never cook a meal, and people seem to lack a clear understanding of how to achieve these values. I call this collection of contradictions the *American Paradox*, and I wrote *Pace of Provence* to help resolve that paradox.

I can imagine your surprise at that idea of eating in the French way and remaining healthy. "Don't the French eat butter, cream, and cheese every day?" you ask.

Well, yes, you are right, the "classic" French cuisine can be unhealthy, loaded with saturated fats, too much meat, and too much alcohol. A typical robust lunch in a good restaurant might be foie gras, roast duck with orange sauce, green beans, cheese, pastry, all of this washed down with a bottle of Cahors or Bourgogne. After a shot of espresso, the happy customers might then slowly sip a glass of poire William (a pear eau-de-vie from southwestern France), and stay at the table, totally satisfied and relaxed, talking and laughing, for another hour.

And yet the French live as long a life as people from other nations and die with no unusual diet-induced maladies. In fact, the incidence of coronary heart disease is generally lower in France.[1] The French are nowhere near as overweight as many

---

1. The incidence of coronary heart disease is also strikingly lower in France compared to other developed countries, excluding Japan. This seems strange if we assume that consumption of cholesterol and saturated animal fats is a leading cause for coronary heart disease. But in reality, the nature of the causal links between cholesterol and fat in the diet and coronary heart disease remain obscure. There are many unexplained factors: 50 to 60 percent of patients with heart disease do not have elevated cholesterol counts. Many groups with extremely high animal fat and cholesterol diets, such as the Eskimos and the Laps, have lower than expected rates of cardiovascular disease. (Harris Marvin. The sacred cow and the abominable pig. Simon & Schuster. NY 1987)

Americans. I call this the *French Paradox*. Why aren't the French poisoned by excess as often as people from other countries are? How do they do it?

A single reason for the *French Paradox* was revealed in Dr. St. Leger's article in an issue of The Lancet in1979, relating red wine consumption to low heart disease rates in the western countries. Wine-drinking countries such as France or Italy score at the bottom of the list. This raises the question: is it the wine only that has such a beneficial effect on heart health? The answer, I think, is no. Health and longevity have a great deal to do with French lifestyle in general, with the manner in which the French think about and consume their food, and the way they make eating even the simplest meal into an occasion. The French have a passion for living well—l'art de vivre, we call it—with high-quality food being an essential component of that life. People make time for their meals, they eat together regularly, they enjoy working in the kitchen, and most of all, they delight in the act of eating.

The idea of *Pace of Provence* is simple: take the best of the French diet and adapt it to our modern American concerns about how to eat both well and healthy. I will share with you the strategies that work for me: how I organize, plan and shop for high-quality meals, reserve the time to cook and eat them, and still find ways to relax.

I prefer to try a new recipe when I have time, am in the mood for cooking, and am not expecting guests. I read the recipe several times before I start, even though I am eager to begin. When I am familiar with the recipe and its various steps, I measure the ingredients, cutting and chopping them as required. Next I stop for a minute and relax; I consider I am now half done. If I keep my attention concentrated, the rest of the work usually goes smoothly, but you must keep in mind that a recipe is not a magic formula that works uniformly under all circumstances. There are many variables (climate, quality of ingredients, the cook's level of skill), so don't expect perfection the first time. After finishing, I write notes indicating what worked and what didn't and adapt the recipe accordingly the next time I make it.

I encourage you to be free and creative when you cook. Please consider it your right and duty to modify any recipe you find here once you have succeeded in making it. For example, try the "Classic all-purpose French sauce"* and innovate according to your taste and mood. Little by little, you will learn to cook instinctively by smell and taste.

This is what I find so exciting about cooking: making new, creative dishes every day for the enjoyment of everyone around me and for myself.

Yolande Matoré Hoisington

In the course of 20 years of living and working in the United States, I have learned a lot about this country's customs and habits. As a mother, a cook, and a health counselor, I have experienced, observed, and compared the advantages, the particularities, and the constraints of eating and living in both countries.

In France, for most girls, learning to cook is an important part of their upbringing. I was not so lucky. My father, who came from a traditional French family, met my mother in Lithuania, where he was a faculty instructor in the French department of the university, just before World War II. They married after the war and settled in Paris.

Lithuanians do not share the French emphasis on food preparation and mealtime. My mother, although she cooked special meals occasionally when we had guests or a family picnic, never became enthusiastic about planning and preparing the family meals despite my father's encouragements. Her food was healthy but boring. I remember having almost the same meal for lunch and dinner every day: tomatoes, cucumber, radishes, broiled steak or fish, canned green beans or peas, and cheese or yogurt for dessert.

I felt, during my youth, probably under the influence of the French side of my family, that I was missing out on something important: the cultivation of a taste for and enjoyment of fine food.

After my university education, I had my own apartment in Paris and lived by myself for several years. This time seemed the perfect opportunity to investigate cooking. I experimented with new ingredients, new tastes, new cooking techniques. My curiosity was endless. At first, I enjoyed cooking from recipes when I had friends coming over. Soon planning meals and cooking on a daily basis became a way for me to educate myself about good food habits, improve my lifestyle, and feel more in control of my life. I never regretted the effort it took.

Working in Paris as a clinical psychologist, I was fascinated by the mysterious connections between emotions, eating, and health. My professional focus was on psychosomatic medicine: how and why people get sick. One day, I met an American postgraduate dental student, William Hoisington, specializing in periodontics. Talking together was difficult at first because his French was basic and my English was nonexistent! Yet I discovered that we shared common interests and the belief that lifestyle habits play a great role in health. We thought it would be exciting and potentially rewarding if we combined our two approaches—medical and psycho-nutritional—to gain a perspective on better healing.

Later, we married and decided to live in Seattle. William opened an office in which to practice his non-invasive treatment called TIP—Tri-Immuno-Phasic periodontal therapy—which he conceived and developed during many years of study and practice in Europe and the United States. This treatment joins the sciences of implantology, immunology, and, with my collaboration, health and psychological counseling.

Together we built an experimental program called "Nutrition+". I was in charge of instructing our patients about lifestyle changes (according to the French eating principles and the lifestyle concepts I will discuss in this book), nutrition, exercise, and dental hygiene.

Before long, we realized we were getting amazing results. Not only did our patients' damaged gums and bones heal properly, our patients themselves often experienced new and surprising changes!

A 32-year-old woman who was tired all the time discovered she had more energy and no longer needed naps. Her skin cleared up, her hair became shinier, and she decided to quit smoking. A retired schoolteacher found pleasure again in life by being able to eat corn on the cob from her garden, not only because she could chew it, but also because her digestive problems disappeared. As a bonus, she lost quite a few pounds. She now had the energy and fitness to join her husband in his long walks in the mountains.

Surely when a chronic infection heals—by whatever means—the whole body benefits. Diseases of the gums and teeth affect every other system, notably kidney and heart function. But I can testify, through many years of working with periodontal patients who very often had other medical problems that providing nutritional counseling and lifestyle training helped them considerably in their overall healing.[2]

As a result of our successes with our periodontal patients, I developed a program that benefits everyone, not just our patients. I call it *Harmonie*, with the French spelling, because a French spirit is attached to it, and because I believe health is the result of a fine balance (or harmony) between mind and body.

---

2. There is mounting evidence which shows that genetic background only creates a predisposition to illness, and that only a few percent of the difference in health between any two Americans is determined by the care delivered by their physicians. It is primarily the healthfulness of the environment, and most of all how we live, which makes the difference between health and illness.

It is a one-on-one program that teaches people with specific problems (health and/or weight) how to eat well to become fit and healthy. First my clients and I thoroughly analyze their existing eating patterns to see what factors may have caused their problems. Then we examine the way French people eat to understand how another culture deals with food, and to introduce ideas about potential changes.

Probably the most important part of the program is developing strategies specifically adapted to the client's personality and situation, helping him or her build a solid base for making healthy changes. These changes are incorporated into a client's daily life until they become a lifestyle, our second nature.

It is very important to learn how to reduce stress and increase awareness of ourselves. Mindfulness is my preferred technique. Mindful eating helps our body to relax, so we can pay attention to the taste of food.

Although it is essential to relax and ease the mind, that is not enough. We need to begin a simple and easy program of exercise. Walking daily at an aerobic pace can help us develop a healthy and fit body, sleep better, and have more energy in our day-to-day life. Exercise is the last step in my program for achieving a well-rounded, healthy lifestyle.

When I first gave my *Harmonie* clients a few of my recipes in hopes they would be a useful hands-on tool in the cultivation of healthy food habits, I was pleasantly surprised at the enthusiastic response they received. The recipes seemed to fill the void between the kind of *grande cuisine* that Julia Child and Paul Bocuse promote—which is not always concerned about health—and the boring "lite" recipes for dieters. They demystified the complexity of French family cuisine and showed my clients that changing their behavior might not be so difficult and might even be fun. They started to enjoy cooking as a new way of taking care of themselves.

Writing healthy French recipes for my *Harmonie* clients led to invitations to offer cooking classes. Health clubs, social and professional organizations asked me to speak to their members about "eating the French way", and to demonstrate some easy, tasty, and healthy recipes. While lecturing, I gained invaluable information about the real needs of the general American public regarding cooking and health.

I decided to compile my recipes into a book and present them in conjunction with my philosophy of good living.

The French Art de Vivre

Eating the French Way

Là tout n'est qu'ordre et beauté, Luxe, calme et volupté.
— Charles Baudelaire.[3]

The French lifestyle, particularly as lived in Provence, has always fascinated people from other countries, especially Americans. They sense in it a harmonious combination of experiences, a more "natural" life filled with simple joys—the softness of sun on skin, laughing with a friend, the taste of a ripe peach. "*On a tout le temps!*" "We have all the time in the world," says the Provençal in the distinctive accent of the South.

Each day, no matter how chaotic, holds its own simple pleasures: good food, the company of others, the tranquillity of the passing hour. This is called *l'art de vivre.*

The French love to celebrate. They call it *fêter*, which means having fun. Children's good grades, a job change, unexpected good news, any excuse is sufficient to prompt a *fête* and a good meal. The French manage to find an excuse every day.

To a French person, cooking is much more than putting food on the table. Cooking is part of a deeply respected tradition, one so strong that it keeps la cuisine alive in France and helps it evolve, even nowadays, when the French are busier and as stressed by modern life as any other people. The French feel that keeping traditions gives them roots and helps them and their children feel a sense of connection with the family and the world.

French people would never say, "I don't want to be a slave to the kitchen." On the contrary, involvement in preparing the daily meals provides them with emotional satisfaction, a feeling of fullness, completion. Beyond the satisfaction of feeding one's family is the pleasure of expressing oneself through food and in continually inventing new dishes.

The Mood of a Meal

Even though it is "only" a family dinner, French women do not ignore aesthetics when setting the table. They are proud to show their good taste and care for their

---

3 There, all is order and beauty, Luxury, calm and sensuality.
 from "L'invitation au voyage"

family by the table decorations they choose; that is how they express their sensitivity and sensuality.

Dinner takes place in the dining room, even if it is far from the kitchen, as is often the case in France. (Eating in the kitchen is reserved for lunches during the work week.) The French don't spend a lot of time ironing napkins or fussing with silver serving dishes. The table décor is kept as simple as possible. At my home in Seattle, I use heavy, bright-colored placemats that don't need to be laundered very often. I have three sets of easy-to-wash no-iron napkins. Only on very special occasions will French hosts lay out white or pastel cloths requiring special care. And there is nothing more elegant than white damask table linen with matching napkins!

I enjoy serving the food I prepare on attractive ceramic plates created by local artists. These add flair and interest to my table. I go to the open-air market regularly and always pick up flowers for the dinner table. And since everyone in my family likes candles, I buy them in large quantities, much to the delight of my son, who takes great pleasure in lighting them for us. We all take turns choosing relaxing music to accompany our dinner: it helps create a comfortable and refined atmosphere. Voila! Let's enjoy our dinner.

The French consider taking one or two long breaks during a busy day a necessity for maintaining good health. No matter how busy they are, they stop all their activities and take time to enjoy good food. They spend a minimum of 30 minutes at the table and most often stretch it to an hour or more. Time spent at the table is a feast for their senses and spirit, and also a way to acknowledge the cook's effort.

French people believe they need a calm atmosphere if they are to digest their food well. "Slow down and relax" seem to be the key words for proper enjoyment of a good meal. Could it be that the hasty and often automatic way in which many Americans eat causes their bodies to crave more food and contributes to their excess weight?

When I lecture on cooking, Americans often ask: "How do French people manage to slow down? Do they go as fast as Americans and then shift gears when it comes time for meals, or do they generally operate at a different pace?"

In areas outside big cities and in the country, particularly in the South of France, the pace is definitely slower; taking time to relax always comes ahead of professional activity. In large cities, however, the pace is similar to all Western cities; day-to-day life is overloaded with stimulation, noise, and stress. Nevertheless, busy Frenchmen succeed at slowing down during a meal because, for them, eating a meal is like attending a special event. They will keep up their busy pace all afternoon, looking forward to the privileged moment they will enjoy at the end of the day. Thus, when it is time to eat, the French are mentally prepared: life quiets down around them and allows them to concentrate on the chosen activity with relief and delight.

Pierre Pallardy, a French osteopath-dietitian, in his new book *Maigrir* (To Lose Weight), believes that the key to relaxing is deep breathing. By breathing too quickly we open the door to sickness, fatigue, backache, and obesity. He suggests one deep breath per hour every day, and he insists on the necessity of one deep breath before each meal as a physical and mental preparation. His method is simple: inhale slowly for five seconds while inflating your belly and opening your chest as much as you can. Hold your breath for two seconds, turning your head from left to right without contracting the shoulders. Exhale slowly through your nose or mouth for five seconds and continue exhaling by contracting your abdominal muscles for two more seconds. Deep breathing produces a feeling of well-being and relaxes the nervous system.[4] Our false feeling of hunger disappears, and we feel great!

Savoring and Socializing

The French feel it is important to be not only relaxed but also hungry, which is why at the beginning of every meal they wish each other "*Bon appétit.*" Since pleasure in eating is augmented by hunger, the French like to manipulate it, delaying their pleasure so as to increase it. If dinner is not available when they are hungry, the French will wait rather than eat a snack, knowing that a satisfying meal experience lies ahead of them.

By eating mindfully, the French heighten the intensity of their pleasure in food, and often find that they are satisfied with eating less. They call it *savourer*, savoring, which means paying close attention to what we eat. The French formula for savoring is quite simple: small portions, enticing presentation, a focus on food and conversation, and the conscious elimination of other distractions.

Savoring is done slowly. First the French smell their food. (American researchers found that sniffing food before we eat may fool our brain into thinking we have eaten more than we actually have.)[5] Then they allow the food to linger in their mouths, feeling its texture, sensing its aroma. They chew slowly. Then they concentrate on the aftertaste, waiting at least 10 seconds before taking another small mouthful. Savoring satisfies all our senses, enhancing our mood, making room for a little happiness while we eat.

---

4 Deep breathing encourages the production of endorphin by the brain, a hormone possessing potent analgesic properties.
5 Alan Hirsh, M.D., director of the Smell and Taste Treatment and Research Foundation in Chicago.

But savoring is more than just enjoying eating at a given moment. It involves educating our palate and all our senses; it is being aware of our bodies and becoming more discerning and demanding of quality.

Taking time and savoring life is the spirit of *l'art de vivre*.

In France, eating is a social activity. Voltaire, the well-known French writer of the eighteenth century, said, "Socrates gave lessons in bed, we give them at the table."

To eat with friends or family creates a bond, an exchange and interaction of energy. Mealtime is a wonderful time and place for people to sit and talk endlessly. Most French people like to chat about food and its preparation, especially at the table. They delight in remembering exceptionally delicious meals and wines they had on a special occasion in the past. They enjoy talking about what they will eat the next day and most of all, what they are presently savoring. Everyone comments on the flavor, the freshness of the ingredients, the way the dish is prepared. Criticisms are welcomed as a way to improve, and compliments are gladly accepted. People talk about the events of the day and imagine projects for the weekend or the next vacation. Worrisome subjects like school examinations, money and health problems are delicately avoided until dinner is finished.

The French are generally fun-loving and delight in telling humorous anecdotes and making jokes at the table. Along with conversation, easygoing laughter is an integral part of dining, and comes spontaneously as a result of the close intimacy achieved at the table. Intimacy does not just happen. It takes time and a lot of effort to build.

Feeling close to other people—during the meals or in other occasions—plays an important role in the French *art de vivre*, and contributes to a wonderful sense of fulfillment. Furthermore, studies show that laughter and intimacy can also strengthen the immune system and promote health.[6]

A Rich Opportunity for Men

In those households where one of two partners is in charge of the food department, it seems important that the other partner know how to appreciate food. My father always showed such interest in and curiosity about food and flavors that he made us,

---

6 A study by psychologist Sandra Levy at the University of Pittsburgh, as well as a Canadian study of 224 women with breast cancer, showed that the power of intimacy was at least equal to the effect of hormone therapy or chemotherapy on survival. Similar findings came from a five-year study at Duke University Medical Center: happily married patients were three times less likely to die from cardiac disease than unmarried heart-disease patients who did not have a confidant. The benefits of being connected extend well beyond cancer and heart disease patients. California researchers found in a nine year study that lonely people face a much greater risk of dying from all causes than do those with close friends and family (Russel Wild, *Cooking Light*, "The power of intimacy," June 1997).

his children, share his interests and gestures of appreciation. To make my mother feel special, he always congratulated her whenever she made an effort in cooking, commenting in detail on each new dish she served and sharing his observations about why an ordinary family meal had turned out unusually well. He tried never to leave the dinner table without telling Maman in her native Lithuanian—which he spoke very well although with a thick French accent—"*Achiu uz pietus*" ("Thank you for the meal") with a warm smile. My husband, William, along with our son, Julien, prefers to say "*C'était vraiment bon*" ("It was so good!"). It makes me feel really great.

Because French men are gourmets, they enjoy shopping for the ingredients of the dishes they prepare. (We French believe that knowing how to choose the right ingredients is the basis of a good cuisine.) When men shop, they are free to choose whatever appeals to them, and they have fun talking to the various vendors and feel very useful when they carry heavy grocery baskets home. Since treating the family is one of their pleasures in life, they might bring home luscious pastries or the first cherries of the season or some specialty item found that day at the market. French children are always curious when their father comes back, and eager to investigate the results of his shopping expedition.

French men usually have several dishes they cook very well, and they pride themselves on these *specialités*. My father had a penchant for seafood, and he was always in charge of preparing the seafood dishes. He delighted in shopping for the ingredients and cooking them during the weekend. My brother, Daniel, who is a teacher and a musician, is wonderful at preparing *la pâte à tarte*, (pie crust), which he makes in just a few minutes in the food processor. Each time we spend some time together in our family house in Provence, he bakes exquisite *tartes aux framboises* (raspberry tarts), or *tartes aux abricots* (apricot tarts), for which he has a secret recipe. He is also proud of his salad dressing, and we have competitions, he and I, regularly, our children being the taster-advisors!

American men have also felt the need to become more active in family life since they began showing up in the delivery room in the early 1970s. They want to become involved and share household duties. Fathers now experience levels of guilt as high as that of mothers over not spending enough "quality time" with their children. More fathers than ever are seeking to balance jobs and careers with deeper family involvement. They are rearranging their work hours, are more selective about jobs, refuse disruptive job transfers, and assume more responsibility for child care.

I believe that preparation of meals is a wonderful way for the husband or the father not to feel as if he is merely a provider but one who is fully involved in the life and health of his family. And fathers seem to be particularly successful in getting their children's assistance!

Some of the recipes in this book are simple enough that even inexperienced cooks might try them with confidence. I suggest they begin by preparing this simple dinner or weekend lunch menu:

Simple Dinner or Weekend Lunch Menu

ENDIVE SALAD WITH WALNUTS, APPLES AND BLUE CHEESE*

PORK TENDERLOIN WITH PRUNES AND GRAND MARNIER*

BOILED POTATOES

GREEN SALAD WITH LIGHT RASPBERRY VINAIGRETTE*

APPLE TERRINE* OR CHOCOLATE MOUSSE*

Including Your Children

It makes sense to involve children in meal-planning. They may have tasted something at a friend's house that gave them an idea for some dish they want you to try. Take them with you grocery shopping every now and then.

Some American family counselors even suggest letting each family member plan one dinner menu a week, as long as the choices are nutritious. Everyone's interests, desires, and food preferences and aversions should be respected. Respecting a child's predilections does not, however, mean that fast food and dessert should occupy a major place in the menu. Professional opinions agree that the notion of dessert as a reward should be eliminated. The only reward for good eating is having a healthy body and feeling good. Dessert does not have to be cakes and cookies anyway; fruit, cheese, and yogurt are all delicious ways to finish a meal.

Experts stress again and again not to ask children to "clean" their plates: the parent's responsibility is to decide when and where the food is served; the children's part is to decide how much.

Eating together is important, but preparing food together is rewarding as well. In France, when family members do not have direct charge of the cooking, they find it relaxing and fun to "play" in the kitchen, making up recipes, experimenting. There is a great spirit of collaboration around meals; helping out before and after dinner is a way for the family to stretch the time spent at the table. They feel that doing "chores" together is fun (most of the time!), and they also want to show their gratitude to the cook by helping out as much as possible. Children set the table and help clean up after dinner. While the girls are often in charge of preparing one simple dish, often an appetizer or the salad dressing, the boys usually try to escape the work!

Involving children is a way to introduce them to the pleasures and the secrets of the culinary art. It will probably add five to ten minutes to the time of the preparation but it is worth every minute of it. Grating the cheese, making a *vinaigrette*, shaping meatballs, cutting cookies, the potential tasks that children can accomplish are endless. Encourage them to try something. You might be surprised by what happens!

They even could try to prepare a complete menu. A good choice might be:

Complete Children's Menu

— ※ —

CUCUMBER WITH MINT AND RADISHES*

TURKEY NUGGETS WITH MINT SAUCE*

GLAZED CARROTS*

GREEN SALAD WITH VINAIGRETTE*

SUMMER FRUIT IN FOIL*

— ※ —

Parents are very concerned nowadays about encouraging their children to be responsible and able to prepare their own lunch sacks by the time they are about 12 years old. While it certainly seems important for children to feel less dependent and in charge of their lives, I found my son needed to be taught how to prepare a well-balanced lunch, and checked sometimes. Most importantly, I needed to keep a large variety of foods for him to choose from in the refrigerator. He has become aware that his body needs more variety than peanut butter sandwiches on white bread, potato chips, candy bars, and soft drinks, which contain no fiber, very little protein, and lots of sugar and fat.

In America, many busy parents complain that their children don't care about meals and spending time with the family. Some American psychologists don't agree with this interpretation. They claim that young people today have very warm feelings about the family. A major survey was conducted during 1995-96 on teenage attitudes and found that spending time with family ranked as the teens' third highest value. The report concluded: "Our survey seems to suggest that teens would be very open to the suggestion of family activities." [7]

Another study links teenagers' meals to psychological adjustment, and shows that children ages 12 to 18 who ate an average of five meals a week with their families showed signs of good psychological adjustment—better than those who had only three meals a week with their family ("adjustment" was defined by whether or not they used drugs, how motivated they were in school, and how hopeful they felt about their future). "It would be worth looking for something related to meals that promotes adjustment in teenagers. It might be as simple as showing teens that the adult cares enough to eat with them, or giving them a chance to talk about their lives," the author of the study told the American Psychological Association. [8]

Most French families don't schedule any evening activity away from home, because time spent between dinner and going to bed is considered family time. (The fact that people in France eat dinner late, around 7:30, helps to keep everyone together.) After dinner, they do activities together—take a long walk, play ball in the yard, watch TV, play board games. If one of the parents has work or a special project to do, he or she will do it in such a way as to be accessible to the family. For example, my father used to write academic papers and books in his study after dinner. But his door was always open, and he seemed very happy to be interrupted by my mother asking him for advice, my brother wanting to tell him about an event of the day, or me showing him one of my drawings. He considered this time-out from his work as particularly enjoyable.

Sundays, and if possible, the whole weekend is saved for family walks, for special meals that every member of the family helps to produce—a picnic, for example. The French love the open-air pleasures of a meal in the countryside. More than thirty years later, I still remember the excitement of the whole family getting ready for the trip. We'd cook the day before and then pack our picnic basket with a *salade niçoise* and a potato omelet, occasionally a roasted chicken, sometimes a *quiche Lorraine*, and always cheese, wine, with cider for the children. Just before leaving Paris to venture into the surrounding forests—Fontainebleau or Marly—

---

7 Elissa Moses, managing director of the Brain Waves consumer research group in New York, Knight-Ridder. Nov. 1996
8 Study author Blake Bowden from the Cincinnati Children's Hospital as quoted in *Seattle Times*, "Study links teenager's meals to psychological adjustment," Aug.17. 1997

we'd stop at a local market to buy cherries or a fragrant melon and a warm baguette. It was a feast!

How many times have I heard the following comment coming from my overweight clients and friends: "My parents were overweight. They did not teach us healthy eating habits. They simply did not know any better. We seldom had fresh fruit at home and rarely vegetables on the table, yet we always had money to buy candy bars, ice cream, and potato chips."

Clearly, the best way to influence a child to practice a healthy lifestyle is to practice it ourselves. Instead of simply teaching our children how to eat well, it seems to me essential to prepare and share healthy meals so they can make good choices for their own lives. Some of my son's friends have parents for whom dinner consists of either reheating something in the microwave or dining out. While our family sits down and has a pleasant dinner, Julien's friends resort to meals at the nearest fast-food chain. Teaching children the facts about nutrition only goes so far; the most powerful teaching tool proves to be our own habits.

Dr. Bruno Bettelheim, the world-famous child psychologist, summarized this fundamental truth by saying: "Our personalities and values will have much more effect than television in shaping our children and their outlook on life." [9]

Educating Young Palates

"When I prepare a well-balanced meal, my kids complain because they prefer junk food; they believe it tastes good." So say many parents in America.

It seems to me that what children really like is the sweet, salty, and fatty tastes of junk food. The palates of young Americans have grown so accustomed to mass-produced, artificially flavored foods that anything else tastes weird.

We might reverse the situation progressively by having not only healthy food, but gourmet food that appeals to them—yet does not require lengthy preparation, as you will see in the recipe section of this book. It is very comforting to realize that taste is a highly educable sense. The capacity to fully appreciate the complexity of food is refined with practice, or savoring, and it becomes part of our permanent memory. With proper treatment, the palate can discriminate and learns to recognize a greater variety of flavors. Little by little, the liking for fat and sugar diminishes and is replaced by the desire for fresh, high-quality food.

---

9 Bruno Bettelheim. *Freud's Vienna & Other Essays.* Alfred Knopf. NY. 1990

I can testify through my own experience as a mother that as you integrate this approach into your daily eating schedule and expose your children to good food, they will soon know the difference and voice their appreciation.

A Romantic Interlude

Many Americans think that the French frequently think about love. It is true that French people devote much time and interest to sentimental relationships. They believe in the power of the right atmosphere to establish closer intimacy. Eating together is definitely the best ground for establishing love affairs. And sharing a dinner at home is better than eating out. It offers the advantage of not being rushed and allows more privacy. In France, couples decide on their menu on the phone. They sometimes shop together, or separately bring their share of food for the jointly prepared meal. Preparation starts at around seven and goes at least until nine, interrupted by laughs, suggestions, comments about each other's collaboration, wine or *aperitif* tasting, and kisses.

Dinner is served! The table is nicely set, candles are lighted, music is playing. It is now time for relaxation, conversation, and enjoyment of delicious food.

Treating Yourself

Some of you readers who do not live with your families might think planning interesting, healthy meals is something you would do if you were not living alone, or only when you have company. I want to remind you that the issues presented in this book (on variety and healthy eating habits) are just as relevant for single people.

When I lived by myself in France, I organized my life according to my own *art de vivre*. Exercising, shopping, cooking, eating, and relaxing were all important tasks to accomplish every day. Now when I am alone here in Seattle for a few days, or even weeks (when my son and my husband happen to be out of town), I live according to the same principles. And I have even more time to take care of myself through exercise and relaxation.

When my family is away, dinner is my favorite time of day. I can treat myself! Of course the organization is simpler. I shop more often than usual—at least three times a week—because it does not take long and I like to decide on the spur of the moment what I am going to eat that night.

Alone time is a great opportunity to eat the dishes I like best. Glistening *ratatouille* ("Mediterranean vegetable stew"*) with olive bread, seafood dishes, Northwest smoked salmon, paella-style rice, artichokes with goat cheese, sweet leeks with *vinaigrette*, cantaloupe, fresh bread, and, of course, a glass of wine. Cooking these dishes never takes me more than 15 minutes. I try to eat at a regular time, usually 7:30 PM. The dining room table is nicely set, and I light the candles. I extend my time and pleasure in eating by grabbing a good book and dividing my time between tasting food mindfully and reading. I find myself quite often still seated at the table an hour or more later!

Keep Moving

Living in the Pacific Northwest fulfills my passion for nature and my concern about fitness. My greatest pleasure is taking a long walk after dinner (if the weather allows it) by myself, with a friend, or with a member of my family. I feel that walking helps my digestion and puts me in the right mood before going to bed. I also tremendously enjoy hiking in the mountains and looking for blueberries or mushrooms—porcini, chanterelles, and morels.

In France, we walk a lot because cities are overpopulated and there is generally no place to park. People use public transportation, buses, and trains. They have to walk to get to work or to their homes, and that is one reason they are relatively fit. After I visit my relatives in Paris every year, I am always surprised to realize that I did not gain weight during the trip. I particularly enjoy French *charcuterie* (delicatessen) and cheeses, and the unbelievably light pastries that cannot be found in the U.S. Sometimes I forget moderation! But the funny thing is I never add one pound to my regular weight. The only explanation is that I walk all day long. If you know Paris you probably understand what I am talking about. Strolling along the *grands boulevards* or following the small lanes in *St-Germain* is what enjoying Paris is all about.

I learned to appreciate aerobic exercise quite recently, when I became a health club member. Aerobics allowed me to get in better shape and be less concerned about my diet. Of course it was difficult to motivate myself at the beginning to go regularly to aerobics class, but I made it a priority, and little by little, it became easier. It came to be a healthy habit[10] completely integrated in my life. Here I would like to share with you a personal anecdote that casts an interesting light on the connection between nutrition and fitness. When I decided to complement the *Harmonie* program with a few recipes, I planned to modify those recipes I had used for many years, the ones I liked the most, turning them into recipes for light cuisine. I wanted them to reflect the healthful, nutritional principles I expected my clients to adopt.

---

10 Good physical activity causes a diversion in the brain and short-circuits emotional stimulation, thus reducing nervous tension. As a consequence it is easier to slow down and relax even more during meals.

I spent a few months cooking and trying the modified recipes, using myself, my family, and my friends as tasting advisors. My fat intake went down rapidly as a consequence of my new diet. I never felt any hunger—no more, anyway, than the normal hunger sensation before meals. Nevertheless, to my surprise, I quickly lost six pounds without having had any intention of losing weight.

The greatest surprise came later. After a month or two, I realized my performance in aerobic classes had changed dramatically. I now experienced a different relationship with my body. I felt a lot lighter, not because of the loss of a few pounds, but because of an internal energy that wanted to expend itself. I could, for example, jump higher. I became stronger and more resistant to fatigue. My own explanation is that my metabolism changed with a lighter nutrition, although my diet was good to start with. (Another manifestation of this change was the fact that I became more resistant to cold temperatures—I had been chilly all my life.)

I believe exercise also teaches us to listen to our body and hear its messages clearly. Our body is an accurate barometer of what we are feeling. By paying attention to whatever sensation arises, we gain access to a way of knowing ourselves. It is no coincidence that the ancient Greeks, who included athletics in their religious celebrations, wrote on the temple of Delphi the inscription "Know thyself", the Greek definition of wisdom.

Variety, Quality, Freshness

"The discovery of a new food adds more to happiness than the discovery of a new star," said Brillat-Savarin, who wrote *La physiologie du goût*, a treatise about gourmet eating, the first work to treat dining as an art form. Brillat-Savarin knew that variety is not only the spice of life, but actually the basis of a healthy diet. It is also the foundation of French cooking. Variety provides us with a mix of nutrients, thus preventing any dietary deficiencies. By constantly introducing new ingredients, new recipes, and new techniques, French cooks break old habits based on mere convenience and make way for experiment and excitement. For example, I set myself the goal of trying at least one new ingredient each month. Recently while shopping, I discovered an interesting vegetable: kale. I steam it, then sauté it in olive oil. It is an excellent accompaniment to pork. Balsamic vinegar was one of my major discoveries last year, as were the grains quinoa and kasha.

Quality is essential to successful cooking, and the French depend on high-quality ingredients. Very busy and well-known chefs do their own shopping at the local markets in France because they know how to choose the best-quality products. They don't mind paying more to get what they want.

Americans don't realize how lucky they are to live in a country where good ingredients are relatively inexpensive. When I visit France every year, I spend the initial days of my stay in total shock while shopping for groceries. I have a hard time spending $3 for a quart of unsweetened orange juice, $12 for a chicken, and in the middle of summer, $3 a pound for peaches. The only product less expensive than in Seattle is wine!

Nevertheless, wherever I am, in France or America, I do not scrimp on my food budget. I would not pinch pennies and buy cheap jams and jellies, for example, because good ones have more fruit, or buy artificial pancake syrup instead of real maple syrup. I would definitely buy virgin olive oil and not some cheap vegetable oil. In general, choosing top-quality ingredients allows us to use less of an ingredient because its flavor is more concentrated.

The French adore the bounty of fresh food available. It gives life to our meals. I recently read in a French magazine that Parisians now consider the ultimate luxury food to be not truffles, caviar, or *foie gras*, but *les plus petits pois cueillis le jour même* (the smallest green peas picked the same day)!

When I know that a fruit or a vegetable was still in the ground or on the vine a few days ago, I feel more alive when I eat it. It gets me thinking about gardens and being able to harvest my own food. I feel connected to the season and more aware of the cycles of nature. Eating strawberries in June, for example, accentuates the feeling of spring and heightens my anticipation of the joys of summer. When I have not had melon with prosciutto for the many winter months, savoring it once again in late spring marks a special event.

The French are very appreciative of the sensuous aspect of food—its aroma, color, and texture—and believe these qualities are as important to our mental and physical health as good nutrients. They don't believe nature needs to be supplemented. How can taking a vitamin C tablet compare with the taste of a delicious ripe peach, like concentrated sunshine that melts in our mouth? The velour-like texture of a golden-red mango? The sweet fragrance of a cantaloupe?

Before taking a food supplement, the French ask themselves the questions: Am I eating well? Do I eat a healthful and varied diet? Do I know how to balance my diet?

In France, we prefer unrefined ingredients—fresh bread crumbs, homemade mayonnaise, barbecue sauces, and salad dressings—because they are more nutritious. There is a general distrust of chemical additives to food—colorings, emulsifiers, flavor "enhancers", preservatives. As a rule, I avoid boxed and canned items that carry a long list of ingredients on their labels. A fish or a tomato doesn't have labels! Occasionally, the French buy a cake mix or a packaged soup when they run out of time, but they would consider this an unfortunate scheduling slip-up, and would try to manage their time better for the next meal.

French Meals

BREAKFAST, *le petit déjeuner,* has traditionally not been a well-balanced meal in France. It consisted essentially of croissants or a baguette, butter and jelly, and café au lait. In the last 20 years, however, things have changed. Cereals, fruit juices, and yogurt are now present every day on the family breakfast table.

LUNCH, *le déjeuner,* is usually more substantial than dinner. At home or in a restaurant, the French want a complete three-course meal. They feel the need for this long break in the middle of their working day.

Lunch time is a sacred part of the day in France. My father, who was a university professor at the Sorbonne, took the Métro every day from the Quartier Latin to the 16th *arrondissement* (the west part of Paris), where our family lived (a 30-minute trip) to have lunch at home with us. After lunch, he took a short nap, a practice he considered to be extremely healthy. He used to say, *"La sieste c'est la santé!"*—that is, "A nap is health itself." He was 90 years old when he died.

Most of the shops and offices close at 12:30 and open again at 2:30. Serving customers and making money are secondary concerns. The customers are all busy having their own lunch anyway! [11]

At midday, French children have two hours off from classes. They can stay in school, where a hot lunch is served, or come home to eat with one or both parents. During the work week, lunches are eaten in the kitchen, which is often small and would probably seem inconvenient to most Americans. To the French, the kitchen is a wonderful place filled with warmth and good smells, where the family can sit down together and eat well. In a French household, meals are served at regular times daily, and people accommodate themselves to this schedule. Children learn this early, along with table manners. Old people come to depend on it! When we children came from Paris to spend the summer with my grandfather, who lived by himself in the South

---

11 I recently complained to Kate, one of my American friends, about this annoying French fact of life. Knowing how much pride Americans take in their "open 24 hours" stores, I was surprised to hear her say: "I hope it's never going to change in France!" "What do you mean?" I asked her. "I actually appreciate that people make their meals a priority" she said. "I think there is a sense of valuing time that we have lost. Life is too fast here and it is hard to establish a sense of community, upholding the genuine values of life". I then realized my mistake; she was not talking about conveniences as I was, but about something more important for all of us, our well-being.

of France, he would tell us jokingly that after preparing his lunch and setting the table, he waited each day for the church bell to ring the noon hour. Only then would *Grand-père* sit down and enjoy his lunch!

DINNER, *le dîner*, is served around 7: 30 or 8: 00, when the French feel very hungry—once again ready to eat and in the mood to celebrate!

Because the French enjoy their time at the table so much, they don't want all their food to arrive at once. Instead it is served in several courses. This is like having the pleasure of a meal several times in one evening!

Fresh bread does not appear until the first course. Then it stays on the table for the rest of the meal. It is sliced, often diagonally, and placed in a pretty basket, and is eaten with the *hors d'oeuvres*, used to nap the sauce of the main dish, and enjoyed with cheese later on. Butter is never served with it.

The first course, called an *entrée*, is essential. (In America, the main course is mistakenly called *entrée* (entrer means in French "to enter"). Appetizers are designed to refresh the palate, please the eye, and prepare the way for more solid food. They are sometimes extremely simple: slices of tomato with *vinaigrette*, grated carrots, radishes, cantaloupe, or shrimp. They might also be more sophisticated—pâté or soufflé—and are always savored slowly. The important thing is that the first course be served by itself, allowing 10 to 15 minutes between it and the main dish.

Why is this an advantage? Because it takes 15 minutes for the appetite to decrease once you start eating. When you approach the main dish of a French meal after the appetizer, you will not crave as much food as when you started, and you will be satisfied with smaller portions.

The first course is always coordinated with the main course. For example, a rather filling *quiche Lorraine* will be offered before a light vegetable dish, and a cucumber salad may precede a hearty "Beef Burgundy"*. Heavy courses and light ones alternate, creating balance in the meal.

Once finished with the appetizer, the French never rush to serve the main course. People wait, talk, laugh, and drink until the next course is ready.

Le plat principal or main dish usually receives most of the cook's time and effort. Here is where his or her talent and imagination are invested. Sometimes the main dish is even greeted by applause—when it is a favorite recipe or a grande cuisine creation. What a wonderful way to congratulate the cook!

As with the appetizer, here again portions are small so that people can save some appetite for dessert.

Most of the time *la salade* is served before dessert to refresh the palate and help digestion. Usually, it is a simple green salad with a *vinaigrette* dressing.

If you were invited by a French family to lunch or dinner, you would hear after the salad course: "*Vous voulez du fromage?*" *Le fromage* or cheese is always available before dessert for people who are still hungry. Again, there is no rush. Everyone helps to clear the table, and the children set clean plates or bowls for dessert.

DESSERT is served! It will be light or filling, depending on the previous dishes. During the work week, time-consuming desserts are seldom prepared. Instead, after a nice portion of cheese, there will be whatever fruit is in season, sweet cherries from the local market, a handful of wild strawberries, which are tiny, and exquisite ripe and juicy pears William, a variety not found in the U.S., or Comice. These will be served with a basket of fresh green almonds, walnuts, or pungent dates and figs from Tunisia. Children often prefer a *petit suisse,* a mixture of dense yogurt and cream cheese, or a tempting chocolate mousse or *crème caramel* that can be found in cartons at the grocery store. Sometimes there will be a homemade *crème anglaise* served with lady fingers (cookies) or a *cherry clafoutis*, desserts that are easy and quick to make. Sherbet is also a big favorite.

On Sundays and celebration days, there will be a sophisticated creation. It could be a light *soufflé au Grand Marnier*, a custard, or even a *gâteau* (cake) baked with love and care at home or from the town's best pastry shop.

The Bounty of Nature: Choosing Ingredients

I hope you acquire from this chapter a strong sense of the French carefulness, curiosity, and enthusiasm about food, and an awareness of the wealth of ingredients from which French cooks choose in order to achieve a good and balanced cuisine. Of course, I have noted my own personal preferences and tips, and in the next chapter, when you accompany me on a grocery-shopping trip, you will get an even better idea of the relish I feel when faced with all the wonderful things there are to eat. Colors, shapes, textures, and smells of food bring joy to my life, not only because they are connected to the pleasure of eating, but also because they enchant all my senses.

I like to compare food to the large variety of colors on my palette when I paint. It would be such a shame to confine myself only to a few colors; that would not allow a full development of my skills, and the result would be disappointing. For me, health represents a successful composition in which we use the full range of material resources and the flexibility of our imagination.

Vegetables

Usually when people talk about what is healthy for the heart, they dwell on what not to eat. I believe we should talk about what to eat more of—vegetables, for example. Vegetables are not only low in fat, they are full of fiber,[12] minerals, and vitamins. Picked the same day, a vegetable has more vitamins than one kept several days in the refrigerator, and more vitamins served raw than cooked, particularly overcooked!

---

12 Fiber intake declined in the U.S. from 1977–1994, across all age and gender categories, but at an alarming rate among children who have the tendency to skip breakfast. The American Dietetic Association recommends approx. 28 grams of fiber daily. Today it is estimated that the fiber content of the typical U.S. diet is only 18 grams per day. Good fiber intake helps prevent and treat many diseases. Besides providing roughage, a high-fiber diet is associated with a reduced risk of heart disease, an opinion reinforced by the latest study published in a recent issue of *Pediatrics*, Nov 1995. It is interesting to note that researchers at the University of Sydney, Australia, tested how people felt after eating high-fiber foods compared to those high in fat and sugar. The latter proved to be the least filling for the calorie allowance. Patty Lanone Stearns. "High fiber foods win the fullness test," Knight Ridder, Feb 1996

The French eat a lot more vegetables than Americans do—about five servings a day. At lunch, there will be at least two vegetables served. At dinner, our first course might consist of one or several vegetables. A cooked vegetable accompanies our main dish, and we serve a green salad before dessert.

I suspect Americans dislike vegetables because so often they are prepared poorly. Until he was exposed to the French way of choosing and cooking vegetables, my husband ate mostly corn and potatoes. He complained that the others were overcooked, dry, and boring. Improving the variety of vegetables will improve your health.

ARTICHOKES, cooked then chilled, are served in France as an appetizer. Eating them is a slow ritual: each petal is plucked from the stem, one by one, its soft bottom part dipped in a *vinaigrette* dressing. I usually add one teaspoon of Dijon mustard to my regular *vinaigrette* to make it stronger and creamier. Since half an artichoke makes a perfect serving size, cut the artichokes lengthwise before or after cooking. (This also allows us to eat artichokes more often, as they can be quite costly).

ASPARAGUS in season should be high on your list of what we call in France *cuisine légère*, "light cooking." It is rich in fiber and an excellent stimulant to the digestive system. Served still warm with a "Light raspberry vinaigrette"*, it makes one of the best appetizers in spring.

BEETS are a great addition to the *plat de crudités*, or vegetable platter. They add color, flavor, and lots of minerals, and are easy to cook. You can bake them for one hour at 400° after wrapping them in aluminum foil. I personally prefer to boil them for 45 minutes in water to which I add two tablespoons of sugar. Beets are delicious and keep very well unpeeled in the refrigerator, always ready for use.

BELGIAN ENDIVE is a winter salad of France. Look for small, oval-shaped, pale yellow heads. Try it dressed in a strong mustardy vinaigrette with blue cheese (Roquefort), walnuts, and apples. This is a nourishing main course for lunch if you serve slices of whole wheat bread with it and yogurt with light cookies for dessert.

CRUCIFEROUS VEGETABLES such as broccoli, cauliflower, Brussels sprouts, kale, turnips, and cabbage are rich in water, fibers, and vitamin C, and are also a major source of vitamin A.

In France, we steam the whole cauliflower, chill it, and serve it as an appetizer. I like to surround it with tomatoes, then garnish it with chopped parsley. A few black olives, the small *niçoises* are my favorite, add a nice touch of color to this pretty dish. I serve a thick, mustardy vinaigrette separately in a serving bowl.

GARLIC has been receiving increased scientific attention recently. Research has shown that it benefits the cardiovascular system. No wonder that Greek athletes ate garlic before their competitions! The French have believed in the virtues of garlic since the beginning of the art of cooking. My grandfather chewed three raw garlic cloves every morning! He was convinced of its strengthening and preventive power. I don't know if he was right about garlic, but he lived a long, healthy and wonderful life.

GREEN SALAD in France, is a tasty course served by itself. It is important for digestive purposes, since the chewing required to eat salad restimulates saliva flow, and the greens themselves add bulk in the digestive system, providing more time for the body's absorption of nutrients. French people consider *la salade* a symbol of health. The darker the green, the better the source of vitamins. A meal does not seem complete without it.

Wild leaves have become a very popular salad. You might add *arugula* leaves, also called rocket, to your salad bowl. This green plant with dark leaves has a pungent, peppery flavor. *Radicchio* looks like a small, purplish cabbage. It is slightly bitter, has crisp leaves, and provides color and flavor in salads. One small head of radicchio will suffice for at least three salads. Why not try watercress? This salad green is very popular in France and garnishes many meat dishes. It is sold in bunches. The small green leaves have a spicy flavor that adds variety to salad. Once you know what it looks like and how it tastes, try to find it growing wild along streambanks and by shallow creeks. Be sure to wash it thoroughly.

The French recently revived the tradition, popular in the Middle Ages, of decorating their green salads with edible flowers such as *nasturtiums*. Try it in summer!

LEEKS are found in all French vegetable gardens throughout the year. They are called *l'asperge du pauvre,* the "poor man's asparagus." Cheaper than asparagus but still wonderfully flavorful, leeks are rich in vitamins A, B, and C. Leeks must be cleaned well, since dirt collects in their leaves.

Many French recipes call for the use of "the white part only" in sauces particularly, because the white part has the sweet and delicate taste of onion. Leeks add a unique flavor to vegetable soups, but the way I enjoy them most—as does my family—is steamed and served with a vinaigrette as a first course while still warm.

LEGUMES, dried beans, lentils, and peas, are extremely nutritious and an excellent source of vegetable protein. The great diversity of legumes offers numerous possibilities for preparing delicious recipes the entire family can enjoy.

Try the *flageolets*, a variety of green kidney bean particularly appreciated in France, served with roast leg of lamb. I decorate my lentils or bean dishes with chopped fresh herbs—parsley or mint—to compensate for the vitamins lost in the process of cooking. They also add vivid color to the preparation.

MUSHROOMS that are cultivated are widely used in most sauces and dishes—providing they are small, fresh, and firm. Combined with *crème fraiche* (or with nonfat sour cream in my recipes), they flavor the famous *sauce normande*.

Great cooks also use wild mushrooms in the traditional *Omelette aux cèpes. Cèpes*, porcini, are big, fleshy brown-capped succulent mushrooms. Along with morels, *girolles*, and *mousserons*, they grow in the many cool French forests (as well as in the mountains near Seattle). They are hunted from September through November for the great pleasure of gourmet consumers everywhere in the world.

When talking about mushrooms, I cannot omit mentioning truffles, the black diamond of French gastronomy. A truffle is a ball-shaped fungus about the size of a walnut. It grows on the roots of oak trees. Hunters release a pig trained to scent out mature truffles. Gourmet consumers and chefs come to annual fairs or markets in townships like Cahors to bargain for their truffle supply, often paying a fortune for just a few. Most of the world's truffle production, however, ends up in small, expensive cans purchased from fancy delis.

The truffle's aroma is unbelievably complex and exquisite. The classic method of preparation in great and expensive restaurants is to bake it whole, encased in puff pastry so the truffle's delicious aroma can be fully appreciated. Modern cooks use these beloved tubers chopped, with scrambled eggs, pâtés, soups, and salads.

RADISHES, the young and tender hors-d'oeuvre of spring in France, are traditionally served whole, with some of the green top left on for decoration. They are simply placed on a plate with salt, fresh bread, and butter. (The French use butter during the meals only with certain appetizers like radishes, *saucisson*—that is, French salami—shrimp and oysters).

I still remember the sense of "event" when radishes were served for the first time each year in early May. My father, who loved radishes, bought the first ones available at the market. I am not sure what I enjoyed the most, his excitement or the pleasure I had in savoring these delicate, crisp, red little roots.

If you eat them regularly—I mean in season and out of season—you and your family will learn how their taste varies, helping you to educate your palates as to freshness, texture, and flavor.

TURNIPS are very popular in France. Their delicate flavor complements poultry very well, and is key to the classic French dish *le canard aux navets,* braised duckling with turnips.

My family likes them steamed for 10 minutes and then sautéed for 15 minutes in olive oil to which I add one or two tablespoons of brown sugar. The turnips become glazed and exquisite.

I urge you to experiment and expand your palate by adding vegetables that are new to you, vegetables that give color, texture, and flavor to your menus. "Mediterranean vegetable stew"*, for example, combines many vegetables and makes tasty leftovers you can serve cold as an appetizer. Prepare vegetable soups during the weekend when you have more time. Good recipes to start with are "French onion soup"* or "Vegetable soup with garlic and basil"*. Take some with you for lunch at work, or serve as a first course during dinner.

Herbs

Experience this: take a leaf or sprig of a fresh herb and crush it between your fingers, close your eyes and smell your fingers. Then smell the same herb dried, taken from its jar. There is no comparison. Fresh herbs are nature's jewels. Chives, tarragon, basil, curly parsley and its cousin the flat chervil, mint, fennel, thyme, rosemary, and oregano … the list is as long as the variety of their scents and medicinal virtues. In France, we use herbs to give more complexity and perfume to a dish, but not to dominate it. Herbs offer the cook the opportunity to be creative, to improvise new dishes all the time.

Most French cooks have their own herb garden so they can enjoy these aromatic plants in their cuisine any time. They are the easiest of all edible plants to grow. All they need is a small space in your garden, good soil, plenty of sun, and a tiny bit of water. Or grow them in containers on the patio or in sunny windows, preferably near the kitchen. Herbs can be started from seed or from plants purchased from a local nursery. Many, such as tarragon and thyme, are perennials; others are annuals.

Here in Seattle, I grow basil, parsley, thyme, rosemary, tarragon, and mint in pots on my deck—my yard is unfortunately too shady. They are the herbs I use most. I plant basil each year; the others are hardy and grow year after year. It is necessary to pinch them back often to encourage compact foliage. After using it fresh all summer, I harvest tarragon in November, let it dry for 10 days, and store it in jars.

I particularly love fresh basil. The aromatic leaves are best used in tomato sauce or sprinkled on vegetable platters. Tomato salad with basil is one of my favorite appetizers in summer. It captures the "flavor" of Provence: ripe and fleshy tomatoes, sweet and tasty, glistening with olive oil and garnished with this shiny and fragrant herb. Many French people think basil is a key to vitality. Picasso, who lived in Provence, used to proclaim its rejuvenating virtues.

Tarragon is also a big favorite in French cuisine. I usually place 3 sprigs of fresh tarragon inside a chicken before I roast it. Then at serving time, I make a sauce by adding one or two tablespoons of nonfat sour cream and one or two tablespoons of stock to the degreased pan juices. I sprinkle freshly chopped tarragon leaves on the sauce and put the chicken back in the oven for a few minutes. *Voilà*! Your "Chicken tarragon"* is ready.

If you buy fresh herbs at the store, don't wash them before refrigerating them, put them in a small plastic container in the refrigerator. You will be surprised at how long they keep fresh.

All the recipes in this cookbook call for fresh herbs if available. If not, substitute about 1/4 teaspoon dried herbs. They keep for years, and you can easily collect your favorites. Except for parsley, mint, and basil, I find dried herbs reasonably tasty. Italian herbs (rosemary, thyme, and oregano) and bay leaves are particularly useful on a daily basis.

Fruit

I associate fruit with some of my dearest childhood memories—those long summer days visiting my grandfather in the south of France. My brother and I used to gorge ourselves on peaches, watermelon, and my favorite, the *Cavaillon* melon, a kind of cantaloupe, the best melon in the world. And figs! White and black…

Before my parents built an addition to my grandfather's house, a gigantic fig tree threw its inviting branches over the house. Fig trees are one of the oldest cultivated plants, found in ancient Egypt and mentioned in Homer; in the Mediterranean area they are as common as olive trees. By the end of July, hundreds of large black figs were fully ripe. My brother Daniel and I climbed the magnificent tree and spent our days eating this marvelous fruit, soft as velvet and sweeter than honey. We overindulged sometimes and ended up with skin rashes!

All of us know that fruit is beautiful, delicious, nourishing, and our best source of vitamins. However, I often hear my *Harmonie* clients complaining that fruit is too expensive and goes to waste most of the time. You can avoid this problem if you calculate how many fruit you need per day (two per person) and avoid monotony by experimenting with a wide diversity of fruit from all corners of the globe. People sometimes overlook fruit's versatility in the kitchen. Here are some fruits you may want to add to your daily diet.

APRICOTS are one of my favorites. Tree-ripened apricots have the best flavor. They are deep in color, plump, and firm yet yielding slightly to the touch. Apricots are easy to eat and great puréed for infants who are just beginning solid foods. I like them poached in syrup and added to vanilla ice cream. Try my recipe "Summer fruit with rum in foil"*. It is easy to prepare and delicious.

GRAPES are considered a "wonder food" in France. They help to cleanse the body of old toxic material. It is not uncommon for French people to go on what they call the "grape cure" and use grapes as their sole diet for many days during the grape harvest season. The low incidence of cancer in theses areas has been attributed to the high percentage of grapes in the daily diet.
Grapes are now available year-round. Whatever the variety, look for the firm berries well attached to the stems. I like American grapes because they are flavorful and most of the time seedless, Thompson Seedless particularly are delicious and so convenient to eat before a work out. I also love Concord grapes, although not easy to find; despite their seeds and thick skins I find their flavor divine. See "Grape pudding"*.

KIWIS are a great addition to a fruit salad. Its jade green flesh, with small black seeds, is strikingly beautiful. The fruit must be purchased very firm and left at room temperature until lightly softened. Kiwis are very high in vitamin C. I always suggest to my clients they offer them regularly in winter to the children. Kiwis are easy to eat. Cut in half lengthwise and eat with a spoon right of the shell. Try "Baked fruit with Zabaglione"*.

MANGOES are by far my favorite fruit. I will always remember my father bringing back mangoes from New Caledonia every year in February (he organized a continuing education program for French teachers from the area). At that time, mangoes were unknown in France. It was a feast!
To chose a ripe mango, go by scent and touch. It should feel soft. Avoid black spots on the skin that indicate overripe fruit. They are messy to eat, but that is part of the pleasure of eating this wonderful fruit so well celebrated by Gauguin.

ORANGES, along with grapes, are one of the oldest fruit known in the history of cultivation. Choose the first oranges of the season, for they are the richest in mineral values. If you pack a lunch bag, include an orange. Here's a tip on how to eat it without creating a mess: cut a circle at the top and the bottom and slice vertically along the side several times, inserting the knife just until it's through the skin. Now it will be easy for you or your children to peel it at lunch time.

SATSUMAS or *Clementines* look like small oranges with a soft skin. They are seedless, sweet, and easy to peel, which makes them excellent for children. Like oranges, they are the best source of vitamin C. Unfortunately, satsumas are found on the food markets only during winter, from November to February. Don't miss them!

Buy fresh-picked fruit whenever possible. In any case, select fruit that is soft, sweet, aromatic, and succulent. The French buy only beautiful and ready-to-eat fruit. Unripe pears or peaches are seldom seen in the shops because nobody would buy them. A basket of fruit is a common French table decoration, and it is always passed around at dessert time.

To begin adding more fruit to your diet, try eating one serving regularly each morning, in addition to or instead of fruit juice, (whole, unpeeled fruit has more fiber), and eat another serving as an appetizer—cantaloupe, for example. Also try some tasty recipes that include fruit, such as "Figs with melted goat cheese"*, or "Endive salad with walnuts, apple and bleu cheese"*. For dessert, enjoy a fruit salad or "Pears in wine"* or "Normandy sautéed apples with Calvados"*.

You might want to copy one of my family's customs. My husband loves fruit. "Fruit is the sunshine of the tastebuds!" he often says, and our son Julien shares his enthusiasm. Every night an hour or two after dinner, William prepares a fruit plate. He slices an orange, an apple, kiwis, grapes, walnuts in their shells or whatever else is in season, arranges the slices gracefully on a pretty serving dish, and offers it to the family. Everybody likes it because there is variety and choice, and it is great to spend another ten minutes together at the end of the day!

Fish

The French love fish and shellfish. The coastal regions have long produced an ample supply that is trucked daily to local markets throughout the country. Many of the fish found in European waters are not available in the U.S. My favorite is turbot, one of the largest of the flat fish and highly priced. In texture and flavor it resembles the American halibut. *Turbot à l'oseille* is a delicious dish—broiled turbot served in cream sauce with sorrel, a delicious green that resembles spinach with its acidic taste.

In France, shellfish are usually served as a first course and almost always in the shell—scallops, crayfish, oysters, sea urchin. Shrimp and langoustine—a miniature version of lobster—are peeled or shelled at the table and served with fresh rye bread, butter or mayonnaise, and lemon. It is not the custom to serve tartar or cocktail sauce with shellfish as we do in the U.S.

I eat fish or shellfish at least three times a week. It tops my list of low-calorie, high-protein foods. Even so-called oily salmon has fewer calories per ounce than lean ground beef. Fish are rich in vitamins and minerals, and easier to digest than meat. Along with salmon, halibut, tuna, and trout, I buy crab, clams, mussels, smoked salmon, and oysters—specialties of the Pacific Northwest. I recently discovered mahimahi and sea bass, both delicious Pacific fish that I include regularly in my menus. Their dense, mild, and delicate meat can be cooked in every imaginable way. Try mahimahi in the recipe "Halibut with honey and oranges"*; it's exquisite. I special-order sea bass heads because they make a tasty "Fish stock"*, the base of the wonderful soup "Fisherman's soup from Provence"*.

I always keep shrimp, scallops, and squid in my freezer. Even though they are not as good as fresh, frozen shellfish come in very handy when I don't have time to stop at the store on my way home from work. It takes only 15 minutes to thaw frozen shellfish in warm water (still in the package). I sauté the shellfish in one tablespoon olive oil, four chopped garlic cloves, and two tablespoons of medium or hot salsa for five minutes. I cook basmati rice for 20 minutes and serve it surrounded by the cooked shellfish.

Meat

Relatively few French people are vegetarians. They enjoy food and flavor too much to deprive themselves of the infinite variety of recipes that meat allows us to create. They sometimes indulge in eating too much meat. Being health conscious, I believe we cannot eat any kind of meat we fancy. Again, from among all the possibilities, we choose what is best for our health and reduce the frequency of meat in our diet to three times a week.

BEEF, the cuts, flavor, and quality of red meat in France are not the same as in the U.S. Because there is less grazing land, the cattle are not allowed to grow as fat before slaughter. French beef is flavorful but definitely less tender, which is probably why steaks and roasts are served very rare (*saignant*) in France. If the cooking time were increased, they would become even tougher.

Though beef is a good source of iron and zinc, it is high in fat, particularly saturated fat, which contributes to heart disease. Although the fat content of beef has dropped,[13] the leanest cuts, like eye of round, still contain four grams of fat per three-ounce serving, compared with chicken breast at three grams per three ounces. When I buy beef, I concentrate on top round, top sirloin, filet mignon, and 92-percent-lean ground beef.

LAMB is fatty, but what a wonderful flavor it has! A leg of lamb is a luxury in France, and most families reserve it for special gatherings and Sunday lunches. Roasted with nothing more than garlic, olive oil, and herbs, it is often served with green kidney beans (*flageolets*) and fresh green (string) beans.

I try to choose lean cuts like leg of lamb, serve small portions, and I don't eat it often. If you roast it or stew it, trim as much fat as possible, leaving just a thin film to provide succulence.

VEAL is often served in France and is very tender. French people like *la blanquette de veau* or veal served *à la normande*, sautéed in a Calvados-based cream sauce with mushrooms and boiled potato or rice.

RABBIT AND GAME are healthy alternatives to red meat. They are too often overlooked by those who care about healthy eating. Try "Rabbit in mustard sauce"*. Rabbit is low in calories, and its firm texture offers a nice change from chicken.

CHICKEN AND TURKEY: In France, as in the U.S. chicken is a clear favorite. *Poulet de Bresse* is the most famous French breed of chicken; it is expensive and exquisite. But the French also like to eat goose, pheasant, squab, pigeon, quail, duck, guinea hen, and occasionally turkey.

I always buy top-quality poultry, because I think it makes a huge difference in taste. The best American chickens, free-range chickens, are raised with a modicum of freedom and are fed on non-medicated grains. I serve it without the skin.

PORK: The French love (too much!) *la charcuterie,* or what we might term delicatessen, and have some of the best in the world. At almost every street corner, there

---

13 About 27 percent since the early 1980s. "Meat makes a comeback" *Mc Call's*, March 1996

A Dear Memory

THERE ARE MANY FRENCH RECIPES *for rabbit, but lapin à la moutarde holds a special place in my heart because my grandfather in Provence raised rabbits, knowing how much we liked to eat it when we came for Easter or the summer. He was an excellent cook and proud of it, and we could expect a real feast upon our arrival. I can still remember one hot summer day: it was noon, and we all sat around the table in the shade of a magnificent olive tree on the terrace facing the deep blue Mediterranean sea. From our chairs, we could see roofs of the city of Menton below us, and in the distance, the beginning of the Italian coast. We all felt tired after a long night spent on the train coming from Paris, but now we would relish our favorite dish. We started with sweet tomatoes and fresh basil from the garden and were soon ready for the main course. As we took our first bite, everyone realized that something had gone dreadfully wrong. The rabbit tasted sweet! Horrified, my grandfather figured out that he had mistakenly used lemon syrup instead of olive oil! Because he was an easygoing and fun-loving character, we all laughed at this culinary misadventure—and we still do every time we eat rabbit.*

Note: *Lemon syrup is commonly used in France; mixed with tap water it makes a refreshing drink. In color and consistency, it is much like olive oil.*

is a small shop offering great variety of cooked pork in various pâtés and terrines. They come in baked earthenware pots or in pastry shells, and in a huge range of saucissons (salamis) and sausages, all attractively displayed to stimulate the customer's appetite. (Anything *truffé*, with truffles, will be very expensive.) Charcuterie is the type of French food I miss the most—French ham particularly. I suppose I should be happy not to be tempted anymore by these delicious but fatty foods!

My favorite pork cut by far is the tenderloin. It is the leanest cut and very easy to prepare. Pork is rich in thiamin and fortunately nowadays is "slimming down."[14] I

---

14 2.5% fat. Improvement in the breeding, feeding, and raising of pigs has resulted in an average of 31% lower fat content than in 1963

vary the way I prepare it—one day with olives and onions, another with tomatoes and peppers, or for a change, oranges or peaches. My son, Julien, loves pork tenderloin and has tried several simple ways to cook it. It makes excellent leftovers.

Eggs

Unlike many Americans, the French believe eggs are part of a healthful diet. Farmers' markets are usually the best place to buy ultra-fresh eggs. In France, charming open-air markets operate year-round, with vendors setting up their stands, usually in the church square, at least twice a week. Old peasants sell *oeufs du jour,* that is "eggs from that same day", and a few other farm products—usually flowers and fresh herbs.

I do believe eggs are a perfectly nutritious food as long as you watch what you pair them with and do not eat more than four a week.[15] French people savor eggs by eating them *à la coque*, soft-boiled.

Julien's Favorite Breakfast

HERE IS HOW I PREPARE SOFT-BOILED EGGS: *In a saucepan, bring enough water to cover large eggs to a rapid boil. Place each egg on a spoon and lower it into the water. Reduce heat until the water barely simmers and cook the eggs for 4 minutes (5 minutes for jumbo-size eggs). Lift the eggs from the water and place them in the folds of a napkin to retain the heat while you carry them to the egg cups on the table. Remove the top of the egg by either slicing across the top of the egg with the smooth stroke of a knife or shattering the top of the eggshell and delicately removing the cracked shell. Dip long, thin, buttered and salted strips of bread into the eggs. In France, we use a baguette, but sourdough bread works just as well. The remaining part of the egg may be eaten with a small spoon. Julien likes to fish out the egg that's in the top shell as well.*

---

15 At only 70 calories each, eggs are an almost ideal low fat source of protein, having 4.5 grams of fat of which only one quarter is saturated. Dorothy Foltz-Gray. "The case of the egg" *Cooking Light,* May, 1998

Flour and bread

In France, there are bakeries on every street corner. They sell essentially pointy baguettes, short *bâtards*, white bread loaves, croissants, and pastries. Baguettes are baked fresh several times a day. When served still warm, they are incredibly delicious, crusty, soft and moist inside. Furthermore, they are very cheap—about 75 cents. This is why the French buy mostly baguettes. Whole wheat, rye, bran bread, and other nutritionally good breads are not produced in large quantities; they have usually disappeared from the bakery stands by mid-afternoon. When I find them, they are often dry, expensive, and don't freeze very well. Exceptions are those made in some bakeries in the large French cities or in famous ones such as Poilane, in Paris, which still bakes wonderful breads in wood-fueled ovens.

Americans should be proud of their fresh breads. My family and I eat different varieties of it almost every day here in Seattle. This is America's golden age of bread. Not since the turn of the century has bread been available in such varied abundance and high quality. Crusty whole wheat loaves, rye bread, tangy rosemary foccaccias, flat pitas, Italian *panes* are tempting me everywhere. Olive bread is one of my favorites, served with a vegetable dish such as "Mediterranean vegetable stew"*, "Nicoise salad"* or hummus. I never waste it because it freezes so well. As soon as I get home from shopping, I split the loaves in halves or quarters, wrap the pieces in heavy plastic bags, and put them in the freezer. When I need bread, I defrost one piece in the microwave oven for one minute or leave it for an hour at room temperature. The bread is then heated (wrapped in foil to avoid dryness) for a few minutes in my toaster oven. (If you don't have a toaster oven, I recommend that you acquire one, because it makes frozen bread taste almost as good as fresh.)

When I bake, I always use stoneground whole wheat flour unless its flavor would be incompatible with my recipe.[16] Whole wheat flour retains bran, the outer layer of cereal grain removed in the process of manufacturing white flour. Bran is an important element in nutrition, providing roughage in the form of cellulose. When a recipe requires white flour, I use a good all-purpose unbleached flour.

Pasta

French people are not pasta enthusiasts as most Americans are. In France, we use pasta, and particularly *les pâtes fraîches*, fresh pasta, as an accompaniment for meat,

---

16 The Wheat Food Council reports that white bread is still the leader in packaged bread sales in America.

rarely as a meal in itself. Although every couple of weeks or so, the French might prepare a large platter of spaghetti and serve it with a big salad, a light dessert, and no
bread. A serving of pasta necessitates, of course, a good sauce. Try fresh pasta with
"Chicken with Cognac"*, "Beef Burgundy"*, or "Rabbit in mustard sauce"*.

Here in Seattle, we eat a pasta dish generally once a week. I always serve a vegetable
appetizer such as a *crudités* dish to begin with. I serve it before the pasta dish because
nobody is hungry for vegetables afterward. It's fun to experiment with diverse ranges of
ingredients to make the pasta sauce. I sauté several kinds of vegetables (depending of
what I have in the fridge) in olive oil: onions, garlic, bell peppers, asparagus, zucchini.
Meanwhile, I sauté the lean ground beef in a small quantity of olive oil until water
completely evaporates and meat is browned. I find it important to stir and crush the
meat while cooking so no large chunks are left. This gives a better flavor to the sauce. I
add the vegetables, meat, fresh herbs, salt, pepper, and one tablespoon of sugar to fresh
tomatoes in summer or high quality canned spaghetti sauce (check the nutritional
information on the label). I cook it on low heat for 40 minutes, stirring occasionally.
For dessert, I usually serve a fruit dish as "Pear in wine"*, or "Apricot mousse"*.

Many of my clients rely on pasta dishes as a quick and easy dinner when they do
not have the energy to concoct a more complex meal. There is nothing wrong with
pasta, so long as you don't eat it almost every day! Pasta and white bread are full of
sugars the body absorbs very quickly, but they are less nutritious than complex carbohydrates like whole grains. I find reducing one's consumption of simple carbohydrates is a good first step toward a healthy diet.

When people complain to me that they are carbohydrate "addicts", I suggest they
double or triple their vegetable intake and eat their vegetable course before indulging
in bread and pasta, allowing at least five minutes between courses. Avoiding snacks is
very important, especially those made from foods high in carbohydrates. For those
who must snack, vegetables and fruit are the best choices.

Grains

A balanced diet requires that we eat at least one form of complex carbohydrates
every day. They are a natural source of energy, as Napoleon Bonaparte well knew
when he told Gaspard Gourgaud, one of his officers and companions at Saint Helena
in 1815: "Rice is the best food for the soldier."

Increasing our consumption and the variety of complex carbohydrates will allow
you to comfortably reduce the fats in your diet. There are dozens of varieties to
choose from. Each type of RICE has a different flavor. Brown and wild rice are partic-

ularly good mixed together. There is also **BARLEY**, which helps lower blood cholesterol. It provides phosphorus, iron and calcium. I love it in soups, added 20 minutes before the cooking is done. **COUSCOUS** is great as an accompaniment to lamb stew or as a salad ("Tabouleh salad"*). **QUINOA**, a grain from South America, contains more protein than any other grain, an average of 16%, compared with 14% for wheat and 7% for rice. **MILLET** is also one of the most nutritious food known to man; it is a complete protein, containing all the essential amino acids. There are also kasha and oats to create recipes around.

If you cook two kinds of grain during the weekend—a pot of brown rice and a quinoa dish for example—they will last for a whole week when refrigerated in plastic containers. They can be served during the week with a little modification—adding green peas, bell peppers, onions, mushrooms, or tomatoes, for example. (Quinoa is delicious reheated in a pan with one tablespoon of olive oil and a few walnuts).

Lipids

Lipids are a concentrated source of energy. Our body needs a certain amount of fats, but an excess—or the wrong kind—can be hazardous to our health.

BUTTER is 100% saturated fat (the bad kind). Nevertheless, the French use it extensively to cook and sauté food, adding butter and cream to sauces, and as shortening in all pastries.

How Do You Recognize a Good Butter?

TO SELECT A GOOD BUTTER, *smell it first. It should have a sweet and strong milky aroma. Nonpasteurized butter is still available in France. It is incomparably good and you should try it if you spend some time over there. Check your local health-food store for raw butter, making sure of the expiration date on the carton.*

Note: A few recipes in this book call for unsalted butter. If you use salted butter, reduce the amount of salt in the recipe.

As I stated in the Introduction, I disagree with this traditional French cooking practice from the standpoint of health and try to use minimal amounts of fat in my cooking. Yet I am French, and because I have always loved butter, it was very difficult to decide not to use it for cooking. I was convinced that its flavor was irreplaceable, which is indeed true. I soon realized that a new, fresher, more exciting taste—one more respectful of the natural flavor of the ingredients—could be obtained by substituting stock, nonfat sour cream, and fresh herbs. I still use unsalted butter sparingly on fresh bread and toast, eating very slowly so I can savor it and truly enjoy its exquisite flavor.

OLIVE OIL is my favorite fat. I use it in almost all my recipes. Several types are available. I prefer "Extra Virgin", the most flavorful kind, for salads. I cook with "Pure olive oil", the kind that tolerates more heat and is also the cheapest. Olive oil is, in effect, a pure fruit juice. Did you know that about 10 pounds of olives are pressed to obtain one liter of olive oil?

All of Provence is covered with olive trees, and in the charming southern town called Roquebrune, close to where my grandfather lived, there is a tourist attraction called *l'olivier millénaire*, an olive tree reputed to be more than 1,000 years old! It is still covered with olives.

People in the South of France believe olive oil facilitates digestion, and they use it extensively. Olive oil is a good heart protector due to its high level of monounsatuated fats and polyunsaturated fats, also called vitamin F. If used regularly, olive oil seems to keep cholesterol levels down.[17]

SAFFLOWER OIL is good to use in dishes where you don't want the strong flavor of olive oil, in "Salmon baked in foil"*, for example. It is even lower in saturated fats than olive oil.

CANOLA OIL, like olive oil, has a high level of monounsaturated fats, believed to be a component of so-called "good" cholesterol.

MARGARINE, chips, crackers, cookies and most packaged baked goods contain hydrogenated fat. It is safer to stay away from them whenever possible.

---

17 Recent research shows that low fat content does not necessarily make a recipe healthful. A tablespoon of olive oil is healthier than a low-calorie pudding with poor ingredients. Robert Knopp, M.D., of the Northwest Lipid Research Clinic in Seattle, recommends that everyone aim for 26% to 36% of calories from fat (between 58 and 67 grams of fat every day if you are eating 2,000 calories per day) and not less. One Washington State study suggests that fat intake that is too low does not provide any additional cholesterol-benefits and may even sabotage your efforts to control our cholesterol. Dorothy Foltz-Gray, "The case of the egg", *Cooking Light*, May 1998

Dairy

Most of us need more calcium in our diet, especially children and women. The recommended USDA of calcium for women is 800 mg. per day, but a recent national survey found that the average daily intake among middle-aged women is only 530 mg. To avoid fat but increase calcium intake, cook with milk that has 1 or 2 percent fat content, and use nonfat sour cream in sauces and add it to soups. Good sources of calcium are dark green vegetables like spinach and broccoli. Nuts are also an excellent source of calcium. We have to keep in mind that we need Vitamin D in order to absorb calcium. This vitamin is found in milk, egg yolk, salt-water fish, or 15 minutes of midday sunshine since vitamin D is produced by skin exposed to the sun.

NONFAT PLAIN YOGURT tastes great with fresh fruit. One of my favorite desserts is "Farmer cheese from Normandy"*. Besides its rich protein and calcium content, yogurt acts as an agent for improving the intestinal flora.

NONFAT SOUR CREAM: In France, we use the dairy product *crème fraiche* in sauces and to enhance cooking in general. Its wonderful flavor and texture (and its fat content!) compare to a very thick whipping cream. *Crème fraiche* could not be found in Seattle when I moved to the U.S., even in specialty stores, so I used regular sour cream instead, since it had the right consistency. It worked pretty well in most cases; its slightly acidic taste could be compensated for, when necessary, by adding a small amount of maple syrup or sugar.

When I became deeply concerned about eating light, I took the easy and rewarding step of switching to nonfat sour cream. This was a new way to keep the great texture and taste of my favorite recipes while adding a surprising lightness to the dishes. Now I always have nonfat sour cream in the refrigerator. It keeps well for several weeks. Try my recipe for "Pork tenderloin with prunes"*; you will have a hard time believing it is a "light" recipe!

CHEESE is an essential food in the French diet, although it's eaten in moderation.[18] In a classic French family dinner, it commands a course of its own, after a green salad and before dessert. I serve it only once or twice a week, however, when I don't have

---

18 Test on laboratory animals by Dr Renaud at INSERM in Lyon, France, suggest that while the butterfat in whole milk is immediately absorbed into the bloodstream, the butterfat in cheese is compounded with calcium and then excreted.
James Villas. *French Country Kitchen*.Bantam books. NY. 1992

About Cheese

Soft cheese

BRIE: spreadable and mild, made from cow's milk. Discard the crust.
CAMEMBERT: spreadable with a stronger taste. Discard the crust.
CHAUMES: sliceable, creamy with a nutty and complex flavor.
CHÈVRE: made from goat's milk. Fresh, mild, and slightly acidic, (chabis type).
Semisoft and aged (log or pyramid type). Hard and aged (crottin type).

Hard cheese

GRUYÈRE, CANTAL: made from cow's milk.
BLUE CHEESE: Roquefort: sharp and piquant, made from sheep's milk
BLEU DE BRESSE: semi-hard, creamy, nutty, and mild. Discard the crust.
GORGONZOLA: soft, piquant, and creamy. Made from cow's milk.

meat or fish for dinner. Depending on the composition of my meal, I serve cheese in one-or two-ounce servings.

The best way to enjoy and learn about the many varieties of cheese—there are 300 French varieties alone—is to taste them when you are hungry, relaxed, and in good company. (Ask the clerk at your local deli for advice and tasting.)

Serve all cheeses at room temperature. Let them breathe by removing all wrappings at least one hour before eating, and present them on a cake plate or a wooden board. (Cheese may be kept chilled in plastic wrap for two weeks.)

In France, we put a small amount of two or three varieties of cheese on our plates. Usually we start with the mildest, placing a small amount on a small piece of bread. Thin slices of a French baguette or fresh whole-wheat bread go perfectly with cheese. Crackers are not appropriate; they have too much taste and are not the right texture. When the cheese has a strong flavor (*Roquefort*) or a dry texture (hard goat cheese), we sometimes put a small amount of unsalted butter on the bread first.

We chew this small amount of bread and cheese very slowly, savoring it. Every bite is an explosion of flavors. As soon as we finish, we sip a full-bodied red wine and wait for a moment—generally just a few seconds—in order to take deep satisfaction in the enjoyment of great food, then we start again. Not uncommonly, when my family has a cheese course for dinner we find ourselves still sitting at the table one hour later. Time has just slipped away!

Stocks

You might ask "How am I going to cook *à la française* if I don't have homemade stocks?" In France, and particularly in large cities such as Paris, women of my generation, with rare exceptions, do not cook with homemade stocks. Modern French people, like Americans, are too busy to do the kind of cooking our parents and grandparents did, and most of the time don't have much storage room in their small freezers. Occasionally, they prepare a fish stock to make a *bouillabaisse*, or a chicken stock to prepare their favorite soup, but that will be the exception.

You, like most French home cooks, can buy frozen stocks, available in deluxe delis or grocery stores. I find frozen veal stock an excellent base for meat sauces. The commercially prepared fish stocks have the great advantage of including whitefish heads as an ingredient, something that is hard to find when shopping for stock ingredients on your own.

I keep containers of two or three kinds of stock in my freezer. When I want to use some (usually half a cup), I defrost what I need in the microwave. It is not costly, because I use very little.

Another option is to use canned beef and chicken broth, and, in a crisis, bouillon cubes, which are packaged by several good companies. I suggest looking carefully at the labels and comparing their MSG content. Clam juice is an alternative to frozen fish stock.

Best, of course, is to wait until you have time and make stock. It is not difficult to make (just time-consuming), tastes delicious, and you can put it into 1-cup containers and store it in the freezer for months ("Chicken stock"* and "Fish stock"*).

If I have room in the refrigerator, I always save the cooking water from different vegetables for use in soups, and for cooking rice and pasta. Why waste those precious minerals and not get full benefit from the enhanced flavor this water can give to all sorts of food?

Condiments

MUSTARD: The French love Dijon mustard. It is placed on the dinner table next to salt and pepper and served with pork, beef, and lamb. It surprises me every time I have Dijon mustard in France how spicy and hot it is compared with Dijon mustard in the U.S. (even the French brands)! Try *Moutarde de Meaux*, which comes packaged in earthenware pots; it is delicious mixed in vinaigrette.

Light soy sauce, hot pepper sauce, and Worcestershire sauce are also basic condiments you should have on hand. They are useful in sauces and add extra flavor to soups, eggs, or casseroles.

SALAD DRESSING: I love salads of all kinds, so I have spent my cooking life improving upon and varying my salad dressings, taking advantage of the large variety of oils and vinegars available at the grocery store: flavored olive oils, walnut and hazelnut oils, balsamic vinegar, sophisticated vinegars like raspberry and strawberry—the choices seem endless. They all speak to my heart.

A vinaigrette, the basic French dressing, is very simple to prepare, and if you really like salads, why not spend the few minutes it takes to make your dressing from scratch? If you make it in advance and store it in a tightly closed jar; it keeps a week or more in the refrigerator.

A good trick for making a light vinaigrette is to replace half of the oil with veal or chicken stock. The result is flavorful and has only half the calories. With the addition of fresh herbs, your homemade dressing will surpass the quality and flavor of a "lite" commercial salad dressing. You will save money as well.

SALT AND PEPPER: I believe that the only way to educate our palates and become great cooks is to repeatedly taste the food throughout the cooking process. When I cook, I keep a teaspoon nearby to dip in the preparation, then I taste it with the tip of my tongue. I add salt and pepper according to the messages I get from my tastebuds while cooking.

Unlike Americans, who use regular table salt, the French use sea salt. They make great claims for it and insist it is as essential to gourmet food as fresh ground pepper. They think it is healthier as well.

SUGAR: In France, sweet specialties abound. Every town features its own distinct variety of candy and cake. *Fruits confits* (from Menton, located in the southeast part of Provence, near my grandfather's town) are brightly colored candied fruits: apricots, cherries, melons, even whole pineapples. They burst with fruity flavor when you bite into them. *Calissons* are a delight for the sweet-toothed: these little oval-shaped almond-paste sweetmeats are made in Aix-en Provence. *Nougat* is probably the most well known candy in France. It comes from a little town called Montélimar in the northwest corner of Provence. It is irresistible! Honey and sugar are mixed together and cooked. Then beaten egg whites are added, followed by almonds, pistachios, and vanilla. The mixture is then cut and dried. Today the town of Commercy is still famous for its *madeleines*, delicious small cakes baked in molds resembling scallop shells and immortalized by Marcel Proust.

Candies and cookies are eaten only at certain times of the day, generally served with coffee after lunch or with tea after dinner. The French savor chocolate and other sweet treats slowly, never eating more than one or two at a time (they prefer to save them for the next day, knowing that the maximum pleasure comes from the first bites.)

In most of my recipes, I use raw, unbleached sugar whenever possible. It is healthier than refined white sugar, since it comes from the initial pressing of sugar cane, which permits some of the natural molasses to remain. I find raw honey and pure maple syrup to be good sweeteners as well.

Sugar is to blame at least as much as saturated fat for arterial degeneration. Refined carbohydrates act with saturated fats to increase fatty substances—triglycerides—in the blood. In the last hundred years, the consumption of saturated fat in America has increased by about 20 percent[19] while the consumption of refined carbohydrates has increased by 700 percent. (Maybe we worry too much about the wrong things?)

If you are curious about how much sugar you include in your diet without really noticing it, read the sugar content on product labels and do this rapid calculation: 20 gr. of sugar (in one serving of cereal for example) represents 5 teaspoons of refined sugar. You can do the same calculation with sherbet—28 grams of sugar equals almost 7 teaspoons of sugar! Check the amount of sugar before you buy cereals, jellies, breakfast bars, ice creams, sherbets, or fruit juices. Compare brands.

It might very well be that when we crave sugar, we are in fact seeking a sense of calm and well-being. Sugar should be considered a mood food. Its consumption stimulates the pancreas to produce insulin, which starts a chemical reaction leading to the production of seratonin, which makes us feel good. Try deep breathing instead; it produces the same euphoria without the calories!

Drinks

FRUIT JUICES: I don't drink commercial fruit juices very often. I prefer to squeeze juice myself and drink it immediately. My real preference is eating a whole piece of fruit and drinking a glass of cold mineral water. (Juices contain too much sugar and

19 Gene Wright, *Sweet Suicide,* Wynwood Press. NY. 1989

lack the fiber contained in the fruit itself.) If you drink canned juices, read the labels. Natural fruit juices with no added sugar are the best.

SOFT DRINKS: A Canadian friend who often travels between Canada and Seattle told me when Canadian airlines are flying Canadian passengers, they stock mineral water and fruit and vegetable juices for breakfast. When the Canadian airlines know they will be transporting Americans, they stock soft drinks!

I really think excessive American soft-drink consumption is a byproduct of American habits of snacking. When people snack all the time on food that mostly consists of sugar or fat, they need a strongly flavored drink to refresh the mouth. Sodas add even more to their sugar intake.

WATER: The French are big fans of mineral water, either with or without carbonation. In France, we have numerous mineral springs: Perrier, Badoit (my favorite), Vittel, Vichy, and many more. Luxurious spas are often associated with these springs, and people come to cure liver, kidney, digestive, and metabolic problems. They are "taking the cure" *(une cure thermale)*. The French don't use tap water very much, probably because they believe mineral water is more natural and therefore healthier, but I suspect they just prefer its fresh and unadulterated taste. A bottle of mineral water always appears on the table next to the bottle of wine during meals.

Water is the main component of every cell in the body. We lose water constantly. A minimum of six glasses of water per day is necessary to keep the body, particularly the skin, hydrated. (Vittel packages its water in an atomizer for use in refreshing the face in the morning. It has been an enormous commercial success in France.)

COFFEE: The French tend to be cautious with coffee nowadays—one cup of *café au lait* in the morning and one shot of espresso after lunch is the daily maximum for most of them. They never serve coffee with meals.

Until about 10 years ago, the French and Italians shared the privilege of being the greatest coffee lovers in the world. Now the Americans have probably surpassed them. Espresso coffee drinking has become an important part of daily life—especially in "the coffee capital", Seattle.

This new American passion has many positive aspects: coffee quality is now comparable to that in Italy, and cozy cafés are opening all over the place, giving people more opportunities to meet and talk. But if the pattern begins to echo that of soft-drink consumption, the American coffee habit could become hazardous to our health.[20]

Wine

Charming, soft, honeyed, fruity, balanced, racy, graceful, round, firm, fresh, simple, seductive, bold, powerful, light, tart, austere, lean, elegant, rich, opulent. These are some descriptive terms used by wine connoisseurs to explain the highly complex taste and the incredible variety of wine.

One of the first things man created, wine holds a special place in many cultures. But *le vin* is the true spirit of the French meal. It enhances the flavor of the food, helps us to relax and therefore facilitates digestion, and helps us extend our time at the table.

Its annual production of wine puts France in second place among the wine-growing countries of the world—only Italy makes more wine—but everywhere wine is made, French wine is the standard of comparison. Thanks to France's great varieties of soil and climate, light white wine can be made in the Loire and powerful reds in the Provence area. Bordeaux, Bourgogne, and Champagne each assemble an unsurpassed wine list.

The French feel that a person of normal weight can safely have one glass of wine for lunch and one or two for dinner every day. But more important than the chemical facts is the way wine is drunk in France—always during meals, in company of family and friends, and under conditions that favor moderation, relaxation, and enjoyment.

Despite romantic fiction, relatively few people in France have their own cellars. In my family, my father was in charge of the wine. As I mentioned earlier, shopping for food was one of his favorite activities during the weekend. Each time he came back from the local market, his baskets full of tantalizing food and produce, he also unpacked a few bottles of Beaujolais (my favorite!) or Bourgogne from the nearest reputable wine merchant (Nicolas), conveniently located around the corner from our apartment.

If the French want to celebrate, they open an expensive Bordeaux. But the *vin de table* they drink every day is usually a *petit vin de pays*, that is, an inexpensive wine that comes from less prestigious areas but is tasty and enhances the quality of the

---

20 Caffeine decreases the amount of water in our body because it acts as a diuretic.
Light drinking of red wine (one or two glasses daily) has consistently been shown to reduce risk of coronary heart disease by 25 per cent. University of Wisconsin Medical School Studies demonstrate that red wine, dark beer, black tea, and red grape juice contain flavonoids that may play a role in preventing sticky cells from forming clots inside of the arteries, a cause of strokes and heart attacks. Dr.Criqui, "Does diet or alcohol explain the French paradox," The *Lancet* magazine. Dec 94

food. It's fun to try different wines all the time: those of Australia, Chile, Italy, Washington State, and, of course, California. It is interesting to make comparisons and to little by little become a connoisseur!

Here in Seattle, when I open a bottle of French red wine, I choose from Côtes du Rhône, Vins du Pays d'Oc, or Côtes de Provence. I avoid wines that carry labels of well-known vineyards; unless you pay a very high price, they are always disappointing.

Brandy

If you don't want to deal with flames when flambéing, pour the cold brandy directly into the cooking pan.

When my recipes call for brandy, keep in mind it's always optional. If no brandy is on hand, prepare the dish without it. If you'd rather not buy a fifth of brandy or liqueur, experiment with a 3-ounce bottle. Then if you like the way the dish turns out, select a bottle of one or more of the following: Cognac, Grand Marnier, Pastis, Calvados. The least expensive brands are perfectly adequate.

Wines, Brandies, and Liqueurs

SPIRITS MAKE A GREAT ADDITION *to the list of ingredients in light cuisine. Cooking with wine, brandy, or liqueurs enhances the flavor of food tremendously. Flambéing might even consume some excess fat, leaving behind the concentrated flavor essences of the spirits used. The best part is that no calories are added except the calories from the sugar if you are using liqueur.*

ALTHOUGH AT FIRST *it seems a bit intimidating, it's easy to master the technique of flambéing. To practice lighting the alcohol, pour a little brandy in a small pan and heat it slowly. When it's warm, lift the pan from the heat and light the liquid with a match, holding the pan away from your face. The alcohol will ignite right away. Pour the flaming alcohol slowly onto your meat, fish or fruit preparation. Experiment first with a small amount of brandy (one tablespoon) and increase the amount when you feel you can comfortably control it. Flambéing is healthy, spectacular, and will add a special feeling of celebration to your meals.*

Organizing the Meals

Shopping

In my opinion, the main reason some Americans have problems with their diet—eating too much pasta or depending on TV dinners—is they don't have the right food in the house. They have not planned ahead and found a way to fit grocery shopping into their busy schedules. To me, shopping is as important as cooking, and planning ahead is the key to a healthy relationship with food.

To this day in French towns and cities, people shop every day. Stores are small and close by, food is always fresh, and people enjoy this daily contact with their customary salespersons, who sometimes are their friends. *Faire les courses*, to go shopping, is an essential and enjoyable activity for the French, whether they live in the country or the city. It is usually scheduled like housecleaning or doing the laundry, except it is considered more fun!

The most enjoyable way to shop in France is to go to local outdoor markets. In Paris and other cities, outdoor markets set up generally twice a week, moving around from marketplace to marketplace throughout the city. There are also many permanent covered markets open every day, as is the case in the *rue de Passy* where my family shopped when I was a girl. French markets are lively places where merchants set up their stalls early in the morning, offer every kind of food imaginable, and begin closing up around noon. Food is ultra-fresh and of high quality. Everything appears in its natural state—for example, vegetables are presented with their leaves still attached, chickens still have their heads and feet on, ducks and rabbits are sometimes alive in cages. Prices vary according to what's in season.

A charming atmosphere of the past and a sense of community still prevail everywhere in French markets and are truly enjoyed by Americans when they visit France. Here it is still routine to shake hands with anyone one knows even slightly, and shopping offers numerous opportunities to do so.

France also has many large supermarkets, American-style. They offer the same variety of products as in the U.S. but under French names. However, French goods sometimes taste different. For example, hot-dogs are made exclusively with pork, and yogurts are not as sweet and have a lighter consistency.

When you shop for fruit or vegetables at a French supermarket, you have to wait in line to weigh all items by yourself on the automatic scale, which often does not work properly, and you are expected to pack your groceries yourself. And there is no help available to carry the bags to the car. Sometimes when I visit France, I completely forget about these customs, and because I am French and don't have the tourist's excuse, people look at me as if I were simple-minded!

I find it wonderful to shop in the U.S., even if I sometimes miss the atmosphere around shopping that is so special in French open-air markets. (I try to go to a farmer's market once a week in summer, here in Seattle. Unfortunately they close during the fall—except for our famous Pike Place Market.) I enjoy the ease of parking and the large aisles in American grocery stores and appreciate the care and respect with which the customer is treated here in America.

I do not shop every day in Seattle. I find it more effective to shop regularly every week, giving it a priority time on my calendar. It is one of the most important and enjoyable activities of my week. I prefer to do it in the morning during the weekend, when I have the most energy. For me, shopping late in the day is a catastrophe; my only thought then is "How quickly can I get out of here?" and I cannot concentrate on my task.

Before leaving home, I consult the family calendar to determine how many meals we each are going to have at home, and how many lunch bags I need to prepare. It is important for me to know the schedule of everyone in the family and have it marked on a calendar. If I am not home for dinner, I must plan to leave a variety of foods for the family. I also take along the list I accumulated during the week of the staples that are in short supply in the pantry—are we running low on flour or raw sugar or coffee?

When you are getting started, you may want to write a detailed shopping list based on menus you have planned in advance. Soon you will be able to create your menus at the grocery store, without having to write them out.

I create the week's menu while I cruise the store aisles. I plan meals while I shop, keeping in mind that each should include:

Meal Fundamentals

❧

1 serving of protein (meat, fish, tofu, milk, legumes, nuts or eggs)
1 or 2 servings of carbohydrates
(bread, pasta, grains, potatoes, beans, raisins, or dates)
2 servings of vegetables
1 serving of fruit

When I enter the store, I start at the vegetable and fruit section. I am attracted to what is on sale, what is in season, and usually organize my menus according to what I see that looks attractive, fresh, and reasonably priced. For example, if zucchinis or eggplants are on sale, I automatically plan a "Mediterranean vegetable stew"*. If green beans are on sale and they look nice, I decide on lamb or beef to go with them. If there are artichokes on special, I plan an appetizer with goat cheese, and so on. I buy a lot of vegetables and hardly waste any. The trick is always to keep in mind the number of meals I will be preparing, so I don't buy too much. I do the same at the fruit section, counting two pieces of fruit per day per person and planning the fruit desserts according to what is in season and what I am in the mood for.

Next I go to the meat section. In my mind, I have already decided about how much and what types of meat I want. I make my final decisions when I look at the price and the quality of what is displayed. For example, if, when buying the green beans, I had in mind serving lamb or beef with them, and then I see some very attractive leg of lamb steaks, I easily decide to go with lamb. If anything appealing is on sale, I plan a meal around it, dessert included. I always buy small portions of meat (about three to four ounces per person). Very often, after choosing the meat and finally deciding all my menus, I have to go back to the vegetable section and add some small items that my meat choice specifically calls for—perhaps fresh herbs, mushrooms, or shallots.

Then I go to the fish section. I like to look at the way fish is displayed and enjoy the beautiful colors before buying it. I buy fish to serve that same day, so it will be as fresh as possible. I ask the salesperson when the fish or the shellfish was delivered; I will not buy unless it was delivered on that day or the day before. I purchase only closed mussels or clams. Mentally, I plan one or two more meals with seafood that I will buy later in the week on my way home from work.

After spending time at the deli section and the dairy department, I finally aim for the center aisles where I spend as little time as possible.

With my list of needed staples in hand, I stock up on them and any other ingredients that are necessary for the menus of the week. If a new item attracts my attention, I read the label carefully, checking for sugar, fat, sodium, and preservatives. Now that I no longer eat hydrogenated fats and have reduced the fat content of my diet, I completely avoid crackers and the potato chips aisle!

When I get home, I write out the menu for the week and post it on the refrigerator. It might look like my **FRENCH MENUS FOR THE WEEK** (see p. 46).

At least once a month, I go to a deluxe delicatessen and supply myself with some varieties of French cheese, fresh pasta, stocks, and also *pâté* (which we eat in a very small quantity as an appetizer).

French Menus for the Week

Monday

LUNCH

Cantaloupe
"Green beans/potato salad with cheese"*
Whole wheat bread
Yogurt

DINNER

"Carrots with ground cumin"*
"Chicken with Cognac"*
Brown rice or boiled potatoes
Green salad
"Chocolate mousse"*

Tuesday

LUNCH

"Vegetable terrine"* with bread
Salad with tomatoes & cucumber
"Crème Anglaise"

DINNER

Artichokes with fresh goat cheese"*
"Salmon Côte d'azur"*
Fresh pasta
"Pear in wine"*

Wednesday

LUNCH

Avocado with light vinaigrette
"Bell peppers marinated with anchovy"*
Whole wheat bread
Dairy dessert & fruit salad

DINNER

Asparagus with light vinaigrette
"Turkey breast with Madeira sauce"*
Rice or potatoes (left over)
"Apples with Calvados"*

Thursday

LUNCH

"Vegetable terrine"* (left over)
"Vegetable soup with garlic & basil"*
Whole wheat bread

DINNER

Sardines in oil & whole wheat bread
"Zucchini gratin"*
Green salad
Kiwi & fresh pineapple with Kirsch

Friday

LUNCH

Leeks with vinaigrette
"Mediterranean vegetable stew"*
Olive bread
Home made apple sauce

DINNER

"Tomatoes with garlic"*
Steamed mussels or clams
Steamed rice
Asparagus (left over)
"Caramel cream"*

Saturday

LUNCH

Beets & grated carrots with vinaigrette
"Pork tenderloin with prunes"*
Steamed turnips
Mango sherbet with cookie

DINNER

"Cucumber salad with lox"*
"Glazed carrots"*
Green salad
"Strawberry molded mousse"*

Sunday

LUNCH

Plateau de crudités
"Halibut with honey & oranges"*
Basmati rice
Apple tart

DINNER

"Mediterranean vegetable stew"* (left over)
Plateau of cheese with French baguette
Green salad
Poached peach in home-made syrup

Planning Meals

It is through cooking that I have come to appreciate the importance of order and planning as a precondition of the daily enjoyment of food and life. Planning means trusting my ability to make wise decisions and follow through on them. It gives me a great sense of confidence and control. Once finished, I can completely forget about cooking for the rest of the day. I feel generally more optimistic and am better able to handle stressful situations.[21]

Every morning, I devote a few minutes to thinking in detail about dinner. I check the list of menus I made after shopping and take some items out of the freezer, such as bread and meat, and put them in the refrigerator to thaw. If there is a large piece of meat, I take it out of the freezer the night before. I calculate the time I need to cook, and think about the ingredients that may be missing.

When I talk with my *Harmonie* clients about the necessity of planning and cooking, their first question is always: "How long is it going to take? I don't have much time." They always seem to be worried about "wasting" time. Cooking and eating are often considered as necessary tasks in order to survive and function effectively (a part of what I called earlier the *American Paradox*).

It is a question of perspective. The French do not feel that taking time to prepare meals and eat is wasting time. We realize that important aspects of our lives and relationships are played out at mealtime.

To improve my clients' planning, I suggest setting aside 15 to 30 minutes a day for a week—preferably the same time each day—to write their ideas and think. Each idea triggers a new idea, the mind wanders. Most people tend to worry rather than think about stressful situations. It is helpful to list on a blank sheet of paper all the activities of the day under three categories: professional time, home time, personal time (planning and cooking being home activities, eating being personal time). Try to balance rather than juggle time. It is important to minimize intrusions upon our minds which require too much time and energy.

For me, leading a simpler life[22] and making space for what I truly value—family, friendship, traditions—is a saner and more fulfilling way to live.

---

21 Researchers at the University of Colorado are now discovering that a sense of mastery boosts the immune system. One group of people was subjected to noise but could end it by pressing a control button they had to figure out. A second group was told they could stop the noise once they figured out the button sequence, but the instruction was false. A third group was told to sit and endure the noise. The results were most interesting: the only group that showed diminished immunity was the one that lacked the power of control. The perception of being in control was as important for the immune system as actually being in control.
–Elinor Levy, Tom Monte, *10 Best Tools to Boost Your Immune System.* Hougton Mifflin C. NY 1997
22 I highly recommend this helpful and charming book by Andrea Van Steenhouse, *A Woman's Guide to a Simpler Life,* Harmony Books, NY 1996

There are problems related to food and mealtimes that every one of us needs to address and talk over with the entire family. Holding such discussions will encourage each family member to feel more responsible and trustworthy.

Composing Meals

In France, a meal is like a piece of music: composed, harmonized, performed, and enjoyed. Each meal has its own melody, and the rhythm and tempo is created by the succession of dishes.

When I build a weekly menu, I try constantly to vary my choices of protein, starches, fibers, and vitamins (I eat meat only two or three times a week). If I eat meat one day, I decide on fish or legume protein for the next meal, and poultry or dairy for the next day.

I also try to balance the nutrients within each meal. If one dish is mostly carbohydrates and fat (lasagna, rice casserole), I not only balance it with a vegetable appetizer and a fruit dessert, I emphasize proteins and vegetables at the next meal.

Depending on the overall composition of the meal, I adjust the portion-size of some of its components. If a light lunch consists of soup with bread, salad, and yogurt, I serve a full cup of yogurt instead of half a cup. If lunch is extremely nourishing, heavier vegetables in a rich sauce, for example, I serve less yogurt.

When French people wake in the morning, the menu for that day (and most likely for several subsequent days) has already been decided, and mealtimes are firmly established. Skipping meals makes no sense to the French. When lunch time comes, people feel hungry and they eat. It is as simple as that.

I often observe that Americans who don't plan a regular time for their meals are always hungry. If you don't think about eating ahead of time, you are going to think about it all the time! I have heard Americans talk about the French being obsessed with food, that they live to eat. I believe the opposite is true: by setting up regular eating times and honoring them, French people are free to do other things with the rest of their day!

The French believe that it takes at least five hours after a nourishing lunch before true appetite returns. They do not snack.[23] The word "snack" does not even exist in French! There is a *goûter*, an afternoon "taste", which might be a *petit pain au chocolat* with a banana, or a yogurt for the children when they come home from school at

---

23 Snacks are a serious obstacle to weight control and good health in general. People consume a small amount of sugar each time they snack, and the need for sugar becomes addictive: they get a sudden burst of energy and then it disappears half an hour later and another hit of sugar is desired. Snacking causes people to think of food all the time, and when we crave sugar, we are not likely to choose an apple over a cookie. Snacking also leads people to lose their sense of what true appetite is. They can't figure out their level of hunger anymore and think they are hungry all the time.

4:30; and society ladies might occasionally have *un thé*, that is, tea and pastries, following the British tradition. But these are the only exceptions.

If we learn to eat when our stomach is empty, we can digest better. A stuffed stomach cannot produce enough digestive juices to break the food down, and so our body is deprived of vitamins and minerals. It may ask for even more food! A healthy body doesn't need to be fed constantly. It works better when there is time between meals, when it can thoroughly digest food and then rest.

Balancing the meals

It is important first to supply your kitchen with plenty of fresh, high-quality, nutritious food. Then you can organize these ingredients into a series of healthy meals.

Let's use my **FRENCH MENUS FOR THE WEEK** (see p. 46) as a point of reference.

You probably noticed by glancing at them I've planned lunches that are more copious than people are used to in America. For one thing, the French more often eat lunch at home than do Americans, and the lunch "hour" is longer in France. The lunch menus here can be prepared as dinner menus if you and your family eat lunch at school or work.

The other thing to keep in mind about these lunch menus is that portions—as with all French portions—are considerably smaller than would be served in America. When French people visit the United States, they are astonished at the huge portions served in restaurants, the leftovers of which are often carried away in doggy bags.

My *Harmonie* clients often ask, "What do you mean by small portions?" Well, obviously, the amount of food one needs depends on one's age, level of activity and body type. But here are the average portion sizes I use when shopping for food.

Portion Sizes

1/2 c. – 1 c. grains or legumes, cooked	3 – 4 ozs. fish
1 c. soup	1 T. salad dressing
2 slices bread	1/2 c. yogurt, pudding, custard, sherbet
4 ozs. chicken	1 scoop ice cream
3 ozs. beef and pork	All you can eat! Fruit and vegetables
2 – 3 ozs. lamb	

Nothing Wrong with Simplicity

If any of the recipes for the meals on the French menu seem too complicated, I feel free to make them simpler! For example, "Tomatoes with garlic"* could become sliced tomato with vinaigrette, the "Vegetable terrine"* could be replaced by an omelet, rice by pasta, chocolate mousse by pudding or yogurt, and so on.

Choosing Among a Variety of Protein

My *Harmonie* clients often ask me : "How can I eat less meat when I have to cook dinner not just for myself but for my husband and my two teen-age sons, who are meat eaters?" Well, I face a similar situation. I have an 18-year-old son, who plays basketball and eats a lot. I always keep a nice portion of a meat leftover or a lean steak and pasta or beans reserved for him. On days my husband and I decide to omit meat, we eat an appetizer and a cooked vegetable course and substitute a cheese course or a seafood salad for the meat course. Since I do not spend as much time preparing dinner when there is no meat course, I usually make a special dessert that night.

Leftovers Are Precious

Leftovers are great things to a cook who wants to be efficient in the kitchen. (I find it most useful to store leftovers, as well as fresh herbs and salad greens, in containers with tight-fitting lids. They keep the food longer and better.)

When I plan a meat dish such as roast chicken, pork tenderloin, or beef stew, I always make enough to serve at two separate meals. I do the same with vegetables, grains, pasta, and desserts. By adding another ingredient, I can create a different dish: roast chicken can become a cold salad, green peas can be added to rice. Some leftovers taste even better than the original dish ("Mediterranean vegetable stew"*, stews, soups, rice casseroles). I count on leftovers in planning my menus. I try to organize, so instead of cooking three dishes for each three-course meal, I have to cook only one new dish, modify one leftover, and serve the other leftover as it is. But be sure not to overdo. One of my *Harmonie* clients gave me a list of all the healthy food she was eating daily. When she brought her food journal, I discovered she prepared only one healthful dish every two or three days and ate it until it was gone. How boring!

Considering the Whole Picture

Lastly, I compose the elements of today's menu based on what I served yesterday and might be served tomorrow. Planning menus is like playing a chess game—in order to make a good move, you must consider your former moves and the ones to come.

Just because I plan my menus doesn't mean I have to become rigid about my diet. I feel free to indulge in some classic *grande cuisine* dish once in a while. Studies show that after an excessive meal, our body regulates itself naturally. It increases its heat production to burn excess calories. We should reestablish our normal weight after two or three days. If we don't lose the few pounds we gained by then, it is probably because we have been increasing our caloric intake for several weeks.

EATING AT HOME

Learning how to combine foods and build menus enables you to change your food habits and create a healthier and more fulfilling lifestyle. Learning to eat well is a gradual procedure. At first, the changes will be subtle, like the light brush strokes that create shading on a watercolor painting. You will make a few adjustments, savor the results, and then make a few more. Everything will fall in place little by little. Soon you will discover your own path, the right way for you alone. Planning more enjoyable meals will then become second nature.

Harmonie lifestyle plan

Lifestyle changes can happen over days, weeks, or months. To help you with these changes, the following are things you can do to make the transition go smoothly.

ENGAGE OTHER FAMILY MEMBERS

Trying to change eating habits is a family affair. If you facilitate an exchange of ideas about health and the necessity of modifying certain habits, you may find that everyone is more willing to collaborate in this important task than you thought. Discuss priorities, how sharing meals together can be time well spent. Do not lecture—instead ask family members to express their feelings and points of view.

You may also want to establish some table rules. I have found that when everyone agrees on a certain dinner time and commits to being punctual and staying at the table until the meal is over, it is much easier to make lasting changes in eating habits.

FREE SOME TIME AND START SHOPPING ONCE A WEEK

Do a big kitchen clean-up first. Get rid of unhealthy and fattening food right away and restock your kitchen with high quality edibles. Shop on the day and time of the week when you are most relaxed. Before you go, check your cupboards and shelves and make a list of the groceries you need to buy for the week ahead. The goal is to keep a great variety of food in your refrigerator and avoid eating out and spending more money as a consequence of not shopping ahead.

Learn to read labels. Food without labels are of course the best ones! Avoid mixes, and buy only high quality bread. Whole wheat bread should be the first item listed.

Freeze items you do not need immediately. Avoid putting junk food on your shopping list. Let your family members buy it for themselves if they want, but don't make it available in the home.

INCREASE YOUR VEGETABLE AND FRUIT INTAKE

Double or triple the quantity of fruit and vegetables you buy to introduce a new balance in the family diet without anyone's feeling deprived or hungry. Always look for freshness and variety. Learn how to accommodate fruit with meat or fish: pork with prunes, chicken with peaches, salmon with rhubarb. Fruits make delicious and light sweet and sour sauces. If you add yogurt or nonfat sour cream to those sauces, you will be surprised by their dense texture and wonderful taste. It is important to learn how to make light sauces because eating plain food gives us the unpleasant feeling we are on a diet.

Menu for the Weekend

❧

*Experiment for one weekend meal with the easiest recipes in this book.
Encourage each member of your family to help you or to be in charge of one dish.
Try for example:*

"FIGS WITH MELTED GOAT CHEESE"* OR
"CANTALOUPE WITH PROSCIUTTO"*
"SALMON WITH LEMON AND CORIANDER"* OR
"CHICKEN WITH COGNAC"*
PLAIN RICE OR BOILED POTATOES
GREEN SALAD WITH "LIGHT RASPBERRY VINAIGRETTE"*
"PEAR IN WINE"* OR "SUMMER FRUIT WITH RUM IN FOIL"*

MAKE YOUR LUNCHES MORE COPIOUS

Rather than eating snacks, I recommend gradually increasing the amount of food eaten during meals. Be patient, for at the beginning, it may seem you ate too much and you are too full, and you probably will feel guilty. Be persistent and little by little, you will find it more natural. After a while, you will discover you do not have to snack as much any more. Each day, eat at the same time (I know it is difficult!). Sit down and relax while you eat. Commit yourself to not eating while doing other activities such as talking on the phone, working at the computer, or reading notes.

Increase your children's lunches also. If everyone consumes more complex carbohydrates and vegetables at lunch, they will be able to wait more comfortably until dinner. Try, for example, "Zucchini gratin"* or "Eggplant mozzarella"*.

SAVE YOUR APPETITE FOR MEALTIME

Being hungry is essential if you want to enjoy your meals and savor your food. On those occasions when you are unable to eat a proper lunch, have a piece of fruit (grapes, for example) and five or six unsalted almonds two hours before dinner, or a banana just before a workout. It helps to lessen hunger pangs without causing you to lose your appetite entirely.

REDUCE THE AMOUNT OF TV WATCHING AND START EXERCISING

TV keeps us in a passive state and encourages snacking. You need to get moving! I recommend walking. It is the easiest way to exercise. The ideal would be to walk every day after dinner, 30 minutes at a regular pace. While walking with friends or family, one talks and laughs, and these happy moments of intimacy extend the pleasure of the meal and create the relaxed mood we all need at the end of a busy day.

Americans are lucky to posses better athletic facilities, health clubs, public tennis courts and golf courses than the French. It seems to me much more enjoyable and rewarding in the long run to decide when, where, and how to exercise than being forced, for example, to climb five flights of stairs or walk four blocks in the rain as the French do. However, a workout needs some motivation and planning.

In addition to walking, start some aerobic exercise—bicycle, tennis, aerobics, dance—three times a week for 30 minutes. Aerobic exercise will help you to burn calories, stay flexible, strong, and increase your cardiovascular endurance.

Three weeks later start to lift two-pound weights every other day for ten minutes. You also need to build muscle mass. Loss of muscle is what transform us slowly from sleek, vital panthers to pudgy tabby cats. The normal loss of muscle with age is preventable through weight training. It is the best anti-aging exercise that exists, not to mention that it prevents osteoporosis.

REDUCE YOUR CAFFEINE INTAKE—NATURALLY

As you balance your meals and add exercise to your daily routine, you will find that your energy level becomes more consistent and that switching to decaffeinated coffee or reducing your consumption to one cup of "regular" a day becomes easier.

FIND FAMILY ACTIVITIES

Start eating at regular times during the weekend. Rediscover the pleasure of eating in the dining room. Don't answer the phone during dinnertime; let the answering machine do its job. Try one "French day" a week—decorate the table, open a bottle of wine, serve an appetizer course to increase the time the family spends together at the table. Focus on eating in a relaxed way and without distractions other than enjoying the company of each other. Make dinner look and feel like a celebration.

At least once a week, play games like Scrabble or cards after dinner, or organize a group project around the house. Remember, teenagers, consciously or not, are very open to family activities. Introduce this question regularly: "What are we going to do together after dinner?"

CONCENTRATE ON SAVORING YOUR FOOD

Here is your chance to practice mindful eating. I like to savor some exquisite food at the beginning of the meal when I am most hungry and my senses are particularly alert. My favorite "savoring food" is fresh oysters. I usually shuck them in collaboration with my son, and we have a lot of fun. I serve them with rye bread, butter, lemon, and a glass of cold Riesling. Oh la la! Try ripe tomatoes with basil and fresh mozzarella, cantaloupe with prosciutto, fresh corn on the cob, lox or *pâté*. After the meal, if you have a "sweet tooth", savor one bite-sized piece of Belgian chocolate that you divide in two separate mouthfuls and eat one after the other. One scoop of homemade sherbet or half a mango are also good choices.

It is essential to serve very small portions and to allow a maximum of time between mouthfuls. Talking about the food we eat also helps us concentrate on the taste.

Try deep breathing before dinner and plan to spend one hour at the table. If the children leave after the meal is finished, stay on yourself or with your partner at the table and enjoy the rest of your wine, or serve a cup of herb tea with a light cookie. Keep in mind that there is strong evidence that the ambiance of the meals promotes health. Discover what the French mean by *l'art de vivre*.

PLAN THREE MENUS FOR THE WEEK

Once you have established a regular tradition of one or two leisurely meals a week, consider increasing the number to three. If you are very busy, start cooking during the weekend and plan at least two leftovers for the following week. Ask your family for feedback on the individual dishes. First try to please their tastes, so they will pay attention to what you are trying to do. Then introduce the necessary dietary changes little by little. The key to helping people enjoy a meal is to make it not only healthy but delicious. This is where the art of the cook starts!

When you feel that this new program has become more natural to you and your family, the next step will be to plan an entire week's menus. Attach the list of menus to your refrigerator after you do your shopping and check them regularly. Menu planning will soon become second-nature to you!

Eating Out

THE LUNCH BREAK

In the provinces, French people often still eat lunch at home. City people, however, like their American counterparts, dine out. Unlike most Americans who grab a sandwich and a soda, the French eat a complete meal, often at the same modest restaurant each day. Here they order a Menu, which consists of a very simple appetizer, a *plat du jour,* and a choice of cheeses or dessert. Most employers give restaurant coupons to their employees, who then add money to it to upgrade the meal and to add coffee.

Here in America, I recommend you find a vegetarian restaurant or a place with a salad bar filled with nutritious beans, grains, and vegetables, and with some hot dishes.

A teriyaki restaurant is a good choice once in a while. If I choose a Middle-Eastern restaurant, I dig into legumes—lentils, hummus, pita, and couscous. I am very careful at Mexican restaurants to ask for steamed tortillas (most are fried). I order whole beans, rice, and grilled chicken. Italian restaurants offer healthy pasta with vegetables or marinara sauce, salads, and antipasto.

DINING IN FRENCH RESTAURANTS

The French prefer to eat well at home rather than cheaply in a restaurant. When they dine out, they go to the best place they can afford. Fast-food restaurants, even if they attract families on the weekends and young people in general, pose no threat to the restaurant business in France. The standard of quality in restaurants is generally high.

Pack Your Lunch for Work or School

LUNCH BAGS CAN HELP *you better control the kind of lunch you'll eat; unfortunately, preparing them is more work! Some of my friends are lucky enough to have access to a microwave oven at work. This makes it easy to put leftovers in plastic containers and reheat them at work. A varied and nutritious meal might be made from leftover beans, grains, or mashed potatoes, a serving of vegetables or a salad, a yogurt, and an orange.*

Coming up with a satisfying, cold sack-lunch menu is more of a challenge. I prepared lunch bags for my son for many years. He loved the salads I put in them , but he lost the plastic containers systematically so I switched to sandwiches. I found that whole-wheat bread with two or three slices of meat and cheese topped with lettuce was a sufficient lunch for Julien only if I added sliced vegetables in a plastic bag, a yogurt, and an orange. I also included nuts, dried fruit, breakfast bars, and fruit juice regularly. A lot of work indeed!

Sometimes, when you are too tired to prepare those boring lunch bags and are tempted to buy disposable lunch trays for children, please look closely at the labels. I feel confident you won't be attracted again!

Before entering any restaurant, French people consult the fixed-price Menu or à la carte list posted outside the door. Fixed-priced menus offer a choice of *entrées*, main dishes, cheese and/or dessert, with wine sometimes thrown in. *Menu* items can be purchased separately, *à la carte*, but they are generally more expensive. In the finest restaurants, dishes are only proposed *à la carte*.

If people are in a hurry but want to eat well, they go to a *brasserie*, which comes from the word "brewery". A *brasserie* guarantees good food, fast service, and a large variety of beers as well as wines. Once in a while when I have dinner at a *brasserie*, I order the specialty of the house, *une choucroute garnie*, sauerkraut with ham, sausage, and boiled potato, served with Dijon mustard. This unique dish comes from Alsace, located in the eastern part of France, close to the German border.

In a classic French restaurant, customers are expected to eat a full meal and to stay as long as they like—all evening is just fine! The service is slow in keeping with the French belief that we should enjoy food at leisure, and it is not uncommon to sit at a table touching other tables. Restaurants are often small and crowded. American tourists in particular seem to delight in this kind of atmosphere.

Dogs are quite welcome in restaurants in France, and nobody is surprised to discover one under the table. If they are small enough, they might be found seated on the chair next to the indulgent owner. French dogs are generally calm and used to dining out!

Unfortunately, there is no water on the table like in the U.S., because restaurants hope people will order bottled water. It is a good habit to ask for *"une carafe d'eau, s'il vous plait,"* plain tap water please, as soon as one sits at the table.

Coffee is served after the meal, never with it. Wine, of course, is the time-honored accompaniment to French food. Many restaurants have a house wine, *une carafe de vin,* which is less expensive and generally of good quality. In the finest restaurants, there is a special wine steward or *sommelier* who presents the wine list and recommends different wines suitable to each course. In this case, a bottle of wine may cost a lot. The French are very cautious about checking the price before ordering.

Even if you decide to eat *à la carte,* you are expected to order an hors d'oeuvre. In expensive restaurants, these are often sophisticated, composed of unusual and costly ingredients such as truffles, *foie gras,* or lobster. Hors d'oeuvres and main dishes are always artfully presented. A vinaigrette is the only salad dressing used.

Cheese (often part of the Menu or served upon request if you decide to order *à la carte*) is presented on a large tray. Hungry customers can choose from 20 to 40 varieties of cheese and eat as much as they want. This is also an excellent opportunity to learn more about cheeses and discover new tastes and textures.

When the time comes for dessert, the French sometimes forget about calories and order incredibly light but rich pastries, sumptuous soufflés with Grand Marnier, or delicate chocolate mousses. French desserts are noted for their beauty, flavor, and imaginative use of ingredients.

Doggie bags do not exist in France because the portions are always small.

Waiters are not in a hurry to remove plates, nor is it considered good manners for them to give customers *l'addition,* the check, before they ask for it. A 15 percent service charge is routinely included in the bill. Customers don't have to leave a tip unless they want to.

DINING IN AMERICAN RESTAURANTS

Although like most people, I enjoy dining out, I must admit to two problems I have with American restaurants: the oversized portions and the sometimes rushed tempo of the service. I also find it difficult to resist temptation when the waiter brings the bread and butter while I am ravenous and there is a long interval before the meal arrives, I find it painful to resist indulging in the bread. Whenever I remember to, I ask for bread "with the meal only," to avoid spoiling my appetite. My solution to the too-large-portions problem is to order an appetizer for myself and try to share the main dish with someone else. Or I choose an appetizer and a small salad. (I can really enjoy my bread at that time!) I order a dessert if I am still hungry. This allows me to satisfy my taste for variety as well. In general, I study the restaurant menu carefully and build my own menu according to the same nutritional principles I use at home.

It can sometimes be challenging to relax in an American restaurant, to forget about time and schedules and to get involved in good conversation when waiters ask repeatedly if they can remove plates (it is true I take my time eating!). Despite all my efforts, I have yet to find a strategy for those situations.

Since dining in restaurants does not help cultivate our eating habits in the way that eating at home and preparing our own meals does, one of my friends decided recently to replace the regular restaurant dates she had with a group of friends with a series of special meals at home. Everyone agreed to take turns inviting the group to their home, and to cook a dinner. They also included a wine tasting—everyone brings his or her own bottle, gives information about the origin of the wine they chose, and the group shares comments while tasting it.

Soups and Appetizers

Soupe à l'oignon

FRENCH ONION SOUP

8 SERVINGS ☙ 280 CALORIES PER CUP ☙ PREPARATION TIME: 20 MINUTES

Soupe à l'oignon is reminiscent for me of my college years at La Sorbonne in Paris. As students, we would find cheap theater tickets. After the show, we went to Les Halles, the center Paris Public Market that no longer exits. The restaurants in this area were open all night long, full of animation and entertainment. I fondly remember dining on their specialty of the house, the soupe à l'oignon.

2 tablespoons olive oil
1 pound yellow onions, finely chopped
2 teaspoons raw sugar
Salt and pepper to taste
2 tablespoons flour
7 cups beef stock or beef broth
5 ounces dry white wine

1 bay leaf
4 tablespoons Cognac, optional
2 tablespoons butter
1 French baguette, sliced or cubed
1 cup grated Swiss cheese,
    Gruyère, preferably

Heat olive oil in a large sauté pan over medium heat. Add onions and cook on low heat uncovered 20 minutes, until onions are a rich golden brown. Stir occasionally.

Season with sugar, salt, and pepper. Sprinkle flour over mixture. Cook, stirring, 3 minutes.

Transfer onions to a stock pot. Add stock, wine, and bay leaf, then bring to a boil. Reduce heat and simmer, partially covered 30 minutes. Skim off the foam from time to time. Taste for seasoning and add salt if necessary.

Add Cognac before serving.

PREPARING THE CROUTONS

LIGHT PREPARATION: Spread bread on an ungreased baking sheet. Toast under preheated broiler until lightly brown.

GOURMET PREPARATION: In a large sauté pan, slowly heat the butter. When foamy, add bread and brown on all sides over medium heat 5 minutes.

Serve the soup in individuals bowls. Top it with the croutons and cover with cheese. Enjoy!

Soupe au pistou

VEGETABLE SOUP WITH GARLIC AND BASIL

6 SERVINGS ❧ 69 CALORIES + CHEESE AND PESTO ❧ PREPARATION TIME: 20 MINUTES

This vegetable soup comes from Provence, in the southern part of France. The warm country climate is blessed by the sun. Long summer days ensure lively vegetables year around. In Provence, garlic is the king of seasonings. Every household has a summer garden overflowing with herbs and especially basil. The pistou, similar to pesto, gives this dish its unique flavor.

1/2 cup small, dry white beans soaked
    overnight in water
6 cups chicken broth
2 small leeks, chopped
1 medium onion, chopped
3 carrots, diced
1 large white potato, chopped
1 stalk celery, chopped
1 cup fresh tomato, peeled and
    chopped, or canned stewed
    tomatoes
3/4 cup green beans, cut in 1 inch
    lengths

2 small zucchini, diced
1/2 cup elbow macaroni dried
2 sprigs parsley, chopped
1 bay leaf
Salt and pepper to taste
1 cup grated Swiss cheese,
    preferably Gruyère

PISTOU:
4 medium garlic cloves
2 tablespoons olive oil
1 cup fresh basil leaves
1 tablespoon cold water

In a large soup pot, bring chicken broth to boil. Drain beans, add to chicken broth, and simmer 40 minutes.

Add leeks, onions, carrots, potato, and celery. Simmer 20 minutes. Add tomato, green beans, zucchini, macaroni, parsley, and bay leaf. Simmer 20 more minutes. Taste and adjust seasonings.

While soup cooks, prepare the pistou. Place garlic, olive oil, basil, and cold water in a blender or a food processor and blend about 30 seconds or until smooth.

Serve soup in bowls. Garnish each with 2 teaspoons of pistou paste and cover with cheese.

"Quelle bonne soupe!"

Soupe du pêcheur provençale

FISHERMAN'S SOUP FROM PROVENCE

4 SERVINGS ∿ 200 CALORIES (WITHOUT BREAD, ROUILLE, CHEESE) ∿ PREPARATION TIME: 40 MINUTES

If you travel in the South of France, you will notice every seafood restaurant boasts this famous classic, la bouillabaisse. This dish is a delicious and sophisticated fisherman's soup, and no French individual would ever spend time in Provence without ordering it at least once. It is the French way to celebrate the true spirit of the south, savoring the delicate harmony between fish and spices. The traditional bouillabaisse requires a long preparation and a special selection of rock fish, particularly the rascasse, which are difficult to find in the United States. My modified recipe is simple to prepare, yet delicious and light. I call it soupe du pêcheur. Try it during the week-end when you have more time, so you can prepare the "Fish stock"* in advance. This dish is nutritionally balanced and nourishing, so you will not need to add more courses. Serve it with a crisp, dry, white wine (Sauvignon blanc or Chablis), or try a rosé from Côtes de Provence. Bon appétit!

1 tablespoon olive oil
1 medium yellow onion, chopped
1 leek, washed and chopped
1/2 fennel bulb, chopped or
    1 tablespoon Pastis or Pernod
Stewed tomatoes (one 14 ounces can)
1 sprig parsley, finely chopped
1 quart "Fish stock"*
1 pound mixed filleted, skinned fish,
    such as halibut, monk fish, Pacific
    rockfish, John Dory, sea bass, or sole

Salt to taste
Pinch saffron
1 recipe "Rouille sauce"*
8 French baguette slices
2 tablespoons butter
Fresh grated Swiss cheese,
    preferably Gruyère

Heat olive oil in a large, heavy casserole. Add onion, leek, fennel, tomatoes, and parsley. Season. Sauté 5 minutes over medium heat.

Pour fish stock in the casserole with the cooked vegetables. Add saffron, bring to a boil and cook, covered, on low heat 20 minutes.

Add fish and bring the soup slowly back to a boil. Taste and add salt if needed. Remove the soup from the heat, cover, and let stand 5 minutes.

Meanwhile, prepare the croutons: In a large sauté pan, slowly heat the butter. When foamy, add the French baguette slices and brown on all sides over medium heat 5 minutes.

Place 2 croutons on the bottom of each serving bowl and ladle the soup on top. Add a spoonful of "Rouille"* and sprinkle with grated Swiss cheese.

Artichauts au chèvre frais

ARTICHOKES WITH FRESH GOAT CHEESE

4 SERVINGS ∾ 80 CALORIES PER HALF ARTICHOKE ∾ PREPARATION TIME: 10 MINUTES

Goat cheese is lower in calories than many other cheeses and easier to digest. It also has more potassium, vitamin A, thiamin, and niacin than cow's milk. Try it with artichokes, which are also an excellent source of minerals. This dish is original, easy to prepare, and delicious. Your success is guaranteed! Some cooks clip the sharp ends of the artichoke leaves off, but I do not find it absolutely necessary. Quark is a German spreadable cheese found in most grocery and health stores in the dairy section. Its acidic flavor and heavy texture remind me of some of the French fromages blancs.

4 medium artichokes, cut in half, lengthwise
1 lemon
4 ounces fresh goat cheese such as Montrachet
4 ounces nonfat Quark or Farmer Cheese*
4 tablespoons light vinaigrette*

1 tablespoon chives, finely chopped
1 fennel sprig, finely chopped, or 1/8 teaspoon dried dill weed
2 small tomatoes, finely chopped
2 tablespoons wine or raspberry vinegar
Salt and pepper to taste

Arrange artichokes halves in a large pot. Add water to cover halfway; season liberally with salt and pepper, add juice of 1 lemon, and bring the liquid to a boil. Cover the pot tightly and adjust heat to simmer. Cook the artichokes 22 minutes or until soft. They can also be steamed which keeps them drier. (It takes approximately 30 minutes.)

Drain artichokes and let cool. Scoop out and remove the choke stems.

In a small bowl, mix goat cheese, Quark, vinaigrette, chives, fennel, salt, and pepper with a fork.

Fill cavity of each artichoke with cheese mixture.

Sprinkle chopped tomatoes over the top of filled artichokes.

Pour a teaspoon of vinegar on each half artichoke.

Serve slightly warm or at room temperature.

Melon au jambon de Parme

CANTALOUPE WITH PROSCIUTTO

4 SERVINGS ∞ 90 CALORIES PER SERVING ∞ PREPARATION TIME: 5 MINUTES

This favorite summer apetizer in France is elegant, light, and very simple to prepare. Because fruit is more easily digested when the stomach is empty, try to eat fruit twice a day, either with your breakfast or as an appetizer. Having a serving of fruit one hour before going to bed has benefits as well and aids in digestion.

Do you know how to choose a perfectly ripe cantaloupe? Feel its texture. It should be firm but not rock hard to the touch and the color slightly yellow. Smell the part around the stem. It should be fragrant and sweet. Compare with a few others, then cross your fingers...

1 medium ripe cantaloupe (1 1/2 pounds)	4 paper thin slices prosciutto, preferably Parma

Cut melon into 4 sections, remove the seeds. Carefully wrap the slices of prosciutto ham around the melon slices. Refrigerate 1 hour before serving.

Serve with a glass of red wine or Tawny port, and savor the delicate and contrasting flavors of this dish.

Terrine de poivrons

VEGETABLE TERRINE

6 SERVINGS ～ 140 CALORIES PER SERVING ～ PREPARATION TIME: 15 MINUTES

In France, we use the word "terrine" to name a vegetable, meat, or fruit loaf. This dish will be a superb appetizer when you have guests. Red bell peppers add a wonderfully sweet taste to this original entrée. It is easy to do and keeps very well. I prepare it a day ahead of time and let it stand at room temperature for an hour before serving. This gives me extra time to concentrate on the main dish the day I have company. You can also serve it as a light dinner with bread, salad, and a dessert such as "Apple terrine"*.

1 tablespoon olive oil
2 garlic cloves, finely chopped
2 red bell peppers, cut into long strips
2 medium size zucchini, cut into long strips
1 medium onion, finely chopped
Salt and pepper to taste
2 teaspoons raw sugar

4 sprigs fresh herbs, chopped, to choose from: parsley, basil, tarragon
6 large eggs
6 butter lettuce leaves, shredded
"Mayonnaise"* or "Tomato sauce,"* optional

Preheat oven to 400°.

Heat olive oil in a medium sauté pan. Add garlic cloves, bell peppers, zucchinis, and onion. Season with salt, pepper, and sugar. Cook 5 minutes on high, stirring occasionally, until lightly browned and soft. Add herbs and mix well.

In a medium bowl, beat eggs together and season with salt and pepper.

Butter a square earthenware terrine or a square 7-8 cup mold. Pour in cooked vegetables. Pour eggs over vegetables, arranging peppers and zucchini on top of terrine, shiny side up.

Place terrine in a pan of hot water. The water should come half way up the side of the mold. In French, this method is called a Bain-marie and is used for gentler cooking. Bake 40 minutes.

Serve this terrine at room temperature or cold if you prefer. Present the dish in its own mold if it is a pretty one, or slice it carefully when very cold and serve on a bed of shredded lettuce.

Serve with "Mayonnaise"* in a pitcher or with "Tomato sauce"* on the side.

Figues au chèvre fondu

FIGS WITH MELTED GOAT CHEESE

4 SERVINGS ～ 100 CALORIES PER SERVING ～ PREPARATION TIME: 5 MINUTES

This is one of my favorite summer appetizers. It is easy, quick to prepare and exquisite if you like the delicate combination of sweet figs and the slightly acidic taste of goat cheese. Even if you aren't fond of goat cheese, try this anyway. The best goat cheese for this recipe is a crottin, a harder type than the fresh goat cheese found in the grocery store but unfortunately, not easy to find. Some delis and health food stores may carry it. This recipe is also delicious with standard goat cheese.

4 large figs or 8 small figs
1 small, round, crottin goat cheese
3 lettuce leaves, shredded
4 red grapes, optional

1/4 teaspoon dried herbes de Provence (thyme, rosemary and oregano)
1/2 red bell pepper, cut into 1/4" strips

Preheat broiler.
Slice figs lengthwise.
Place about 1 teaspoon of goat cheese over large figs or 1/2 teaspoon over small figs.
Sprinkle with herbes de Provence.
Top each with a grape, pushing it slightly into the cheese.
Broil 3 or 4 minutes, until cheese is slightly melted.
Arrange lettuce on a small serving plate, place figs on the lettuce, and garnish with bell pepper strips.

Serve immediately with walnut bread, and take your time savoring this!

Salads

Carpaccio de courgettes aux noix

ZUCCHINI CARPACCIO WITH WALNUTS

4 SERVINGS ～～ 150 CALORIES PER SERVING ～～ PREPARATION TIME: 20 MINUTES

Carpaccio is an Italian word adopted from the so-called nouvelle cuisine. It means a cold dish made with thinly sliced meat, fish, or vegetable. French people are very fond of zucchini. They call it poetically "une provençale à la chair fondante", a Provençal vegetable whose flesh melts in your mouth. It is often used in Provençale cuisine. Zucchini is available year round, but is tastier in spring. Look for small and firm zucchini, which are best for this light and tasty appetizer. For another delicious zucchini recipe, try "Zucchini gratin"*.

4 small zucchini, sliced diagonally
  and almost paper thin
1/2 cup walnuts, coarsely chopped
3 fennel sprigs, chopped

2 tablespoons extra virgin olive oil
4 tablespoons low-fat plain yogurt
Salt and white pepper to taste

Wash and dry zucchini. Cut off ends but do not peel.
Place zucchini slices in medium bowl and sprinkle with salt. Let stand 10 minutes.
Meanwhile, toast walnuts in small, dry pan over medium heat 2 minutes. Set them aside on a paper towel to cool.
Dry zucchini on a paper towel and arrange gracefully on a large serving dish. Sprinkle with pepper and garnish with fennel.
Mix oil and yogurt in a small bowl. Season with salt and pepper.
Pour the sauce on the zucchini.
Sprinkle walnuts over the dish.

Serve immediately with fresh rye bread.

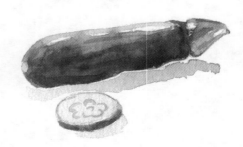

Salade de haricots et de pommes de terre au chèvre

GREEN BEAN AND POTATO SALAD WITH GOAT CHEESE

8 SERVINGS ❧ 220 CALORIES PER SERVING ❧ PREPARATION TIME: 30 MINUTES

This recipe comes from Dordogne in Aquitaine, a region of southwest France. Dordogne is a legendary bastion of French gastronomy. It is the land of Roquefort cheese, truffles, and foie gras. Around the feudal villages such as Sarlat, potatoes are a local bounty regularly incorporated into recipes. This version of the classical recipe is lighter and simpler to prepare. A half recipe is an ideal accompaniment to either chicken or fish.

2 pounds red potatoes, cut into slices
2 pounds green beans, trimmed
8 tablespoons raspberry vinegar or
   wine vinegar
1 cup low-fat plain yogurt
6 teaspoons Dijon mustard
2 garlic cloves, finely chopped
Salt and pepper to taste

Capers
4 sprigs fresh herbs (parsley, thyme,
   basil, tarragon) chopped
4 tablespoons extra virgin olive oil
3 ounces fresh, moist goat cheese,
   crumbled

Cook potatoes in salted water 10 minutes. Add beans and continue to cook 10 more minutes, or until tender.

Mix together vinegar, yogurt, mustard, garlic, salt, pepper, and capers. Incorporate herbs and add olive oil.

When vegetables are al dente (tender but still firm), toss with dressing.

Sprinkle goat cheese on top.

Serve warm, or cold as a leftover.

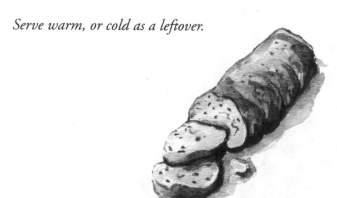

Salade Niçoise

NIÇOISE SALAD

4 SERVINGS ❧ 300 CALORIES PER SERVING ❧ PREPARATION TIME: 25 MINUTES

"La Salade Niçoise" is the most popular salad from Provence. This dish is very nutritious, and the great variety of vegetables makes it quite healthy as well. If you don't mind adding a few calories, try it with anchovy fillets. They really enhance the flavor.

1 pound red potatoes, peeled
1/2 pound green beans
1 small white onion, or
    4 green onions, chopped
1 small head of butter lettuce
1 can (6 oz.) water-packed tuna,
    drained and flaked
16 black Niçoise olives,
    or other black olives
2 hard boiled eggs, halved
3 tomatoes, quartered

6 fresh basil leaves chopped
4 anchovy fillets, cut in half
    lengthwise

DRESSING:
2 tablespoons vinegar
1 teaspoon Dijon mustard
Salt and pepper to taste
1 teaspoon garlic, finely chopped
4 tablespoons extra virgin olive oil

Boil or steam potatoes for 20 minutes or until fork tender. Drain, let cool, then cut into medium slices.

Meanwhile, string green beans (snap off the two ends of the beans) and steam 17 minutes or until tender but still firm. Drain and let cool.

Dressing preparation: In a large bowl, add vinegar to mustard, then add salt, pepper, and garlic. Add olive oil slowly to create an emulsion.

Add potatoes, green beans, onion, and butter lettuce to dressing. Toss until the vegetables are well coated.

Mound salad on a large platter. Arrange tuna, olives, eggs, tomatoes, and basil on top. Place anchovy fillets on top of salad.

Serve with crusty whole wheat or olive bread.

Poivrons et mozzarella marinés aux anchois

BELL PEPPERS AND MOZZARELLA MARINATED WITH ANCHOVY

4 SERVINGS ~~ 130 CALORIES PER SERVING ~~ PREPARATION TIME: 20 MINUTES

This appetizer is an enjoyment for the palate and a pleasure to the eyes. Arranged nicely, it looks like a piece of art. This dish is even better if prepared one day in advance. It keeps very well several days in your refrigerator.

6 bell peppers, 2 green, 2 red, 2 yellow, quartered lengthwise, cored
and sliced in 2"wide strips
2 tablespoons extra virgin olive oil
4 garlic cloves, finely chopped
4 teaspoons fresh thyme herbs or
2 teaspoons dried Italian herbs

Salt and pepper to taste
10 anchovy fillets, cut in half
lengthwise
3 ounces part skim milk mozzarella
cheese, cut in 1" cubes
1 sprig parsley, chopped

Boil bell peppers 6 minutes in salted water. Drain and set aside to cool.

Pour olive oil in a pan and sauté peppers with garlic and herbs on low heat 5 minutes. Season with salt and pepper.

In a large, shallow, oval or round serving dish, artfully arrange the peppers according to their colors (green, red, yellow, shiny side up). Add anchovies. When the dish is cool, add cubed mozzarella rolled in chopped parsley.

Cover with plastic wrap and refrigerate at least 2 hours before serving. This dish tastes even better the next day.

Serve at room temperature or cold.

Carottes au cumin

CARROTS WITH GROUND CUMIN

5 SERVINGS ~ 50 CALORIES PER SERVING ~ PREPARATION TIME: 25 MINUTES.

This refreshing dish comes from Algeria, where people like a sweet and savory combination in their traditional dishes. I serve it as an appetizer with the "Cucumbers with mint"* because of the balance of taste and color.

1 pound carrots, peeled and cut into medium slices	Salt and pepper to taste
1 tablespoon rice vinegar	2 teaspoons ground cumin
1 teaspoon light soy sauce	1 tablespoon extra virgin olive oil
1 teaspoon brown sugar	1 tablespoon parsley, finely chopped

In medium saucepan, bring 2 cups salted water to a boil, or pour 1 1/2 cups water in a steamer. I prefer steaming the vegetables as steaming preserves vitamins and minerals. Cook or steam carrots for 15 minutes, until done but still firm. Drain and set aside.

In medium serving bowl, combine vinegar, light soy sauce, brown sugar, salt, pepper, ground cumin, and olive oil.

Add carrots and toss well. Decorate with parsley for a refreshing finish and extra vitamin C!

Serve at room temperature.

Poireaux vinaigrette

LEEKS VINAIGRETTE

4 SERVINGS ～ 80 CALORIES ～ PREPARATION TIME: 10 MINUTES

Leeks are used frequently in French cuisine. When fresh, their sweet flavor and delicate consistency is purely divine. As a bonus, they are particularly healthy. Try leeks with "Light raspberry vinaigrette"*. You will be surprised how delicious they are.

4 medium or 8 small leeks
2 tablespoons "Light raspberry vinaigrette"*

1 green onion, finely chopped
1 sprig parsley, finely chopped

Wash leeks thoroughly, making incisions lengthwise in green parts to remove any trace of dirt. Cut off the upper third of green part.

Cook leeks in salted water or steam 10 minutes or until tender. Drain and set aside on paper towel.

Arrange leeks on a long, oval serving dish. Sprinkle with parsley and onion, then drizzle with vinaigrette.

Serve slightly warm or chilled.

Concombre à la menthe

CUCUMBER WITH MINT

4 SERVINGS ～ 40 CALORIES PER SERVING ～ PREPARATION TIME: 5 MINUTES

Cucumber and mint are exceptionally cool and delicious as part of a crudité plate. This recipe has a distinctive Asian flavor. Serve it before a hearty main dish like "Boeuf bour-guigon" * or "Paella"* and finish your meal with "Summer fruits with rum in foil"* or "Crème anglaise"* and a light cookie.

1 English cucumber, peeled and
    thinly sliced
1 tablespoon olive oil
2 teaspoons rice vinegar
2 teaspoons light soy sauce

1 teaspoon coriander powder
Salt and pepper to taste
2 tablespoons finely shredded mint
    leaves

Peel cucumber and slice thinly.

In a medium bowl, toss cucumber slices with olive oil, vinegar, light soy sauce, coriander, salt, and pepper. Let marinate for at least 30 minutes, tossing occasionally.

Mix in mint before serving.

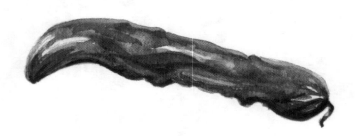

Salade de concombre au saumon fumé

CUCUMBER SALAD WITH SMOKED SALMON

6 SERVINGS ～ 115 CALORIES PER SERVING ～ PREPARATION TIME: 15 MINUTES

This elegant and original salad makes a marvelous first course. It is easy to prepare and nourishing if you serve it with slices of toasted French bread. The quality of the lox makes a big difference in the success of this recipe. Use lox slices instead of "trim", which is an inferior product. To follow this, I would choose a vegetable dish like "Mediterranean vegetable stew"* or "Zucchini carpaccio"* and "Chocolate mousse"* or "Strawberry molded mousse"*.

6 lettuce leaves
2 medium tomatoes, sliced
1 medium English cucumber, finely chopped
1 large garlic clove, finely minced
2 tablespoons "Salad dressing of the sun"*

6 slices of lox, 2 ounces each, cut into long strips
1 tablespoon nonfat sour cream
1 tablespoon shallot, minced
1 fennel sprig, finely chopped, or 1/8 teaspoon dried dill weed
Salt and pepper to taste

Arrange lettuce on 6 salad bowls or small plates. Place tomato slices around edge of each bowl and season with salt and pepper.

Moisten cucumber with the "salad dressing of the sun"* and mix in garlic, then place in middle of bowls.

Mix lox with sour cream, shallot, fennel, salt, and pepper. Decoratively place the mixture on top of cucumbers.

Serve cold with toasted French bread.

Taboulé

TABOULEH SALAD

6 SERVINGS ✦ 280 CALORIES PER SERVING ✦ PREPARATION TIME: 15 MINUTES

This delicious dish comes from the northern part of Africa. It is a complete meal by itself if you add a dairy dessert such as yogurt or custard. It is particularly good in summer when tomatoes are sweet and vegetables are perfectly ripe.

2 cups couscous, cooked according to package directions
1/2 cup garbanzo beans, cooked or canned
2 large tomatoes, chopped
1/2 English cucumber, chopped
2 sprigs fresh mint, finely chopped

6 green onions, finely chopped
3 garlic cloves, finely chopped
3/4 cup extra virgin olive oil
Juice of 1 lemon
2 tablespoons vinegar
6 black olives
Salt and pepper to taste

Place couscous and garbanzo beans in a large bowl. Add tomatoes, cucumber, mint, onions, garlic, oil, lemon juice, vinegar, and olives. Generously season with salt and pepper.

Toss the tabouleh salad and refrigerate before serving.

Salade d'endives aux noix, pommes et Roquefort

ENDIVE SALAD WITH WALNUTS, APPLE AND BLUE CHEESE

4 SERVINGS ◆◆ 180 CALORIES ◆◆ PREPARATION TIME: 10 MINUTES

Here is another opportunity to incorporate fruit in your salad, which is beneficial, as it adds extra vitamins and fiber to your meal. You can substitute the curly endive with a half romaine tossed with 12 finely chopped radicchio leaves.

This dish makes a lovely lunch if you serve it with two slices of fresh whole wheat or olive bread, one slice of smoked turkey or ham, and a dairy dessert such as yogurt or chocolate custard. Quark is a German spreadable cheese found in most grocery and health food stores in the dairy section.

6 Belgium endive or 1 curly endive
1 small apple, peeled and chopped
2 tablespoons nonfat Quark cheese
1 teaspoon Dijon mustard
3 teaspoons wine vinegar
1/4 teaspoon light soy sauce

Salt and pepper to taste
2 tablespoons extra virgin olive oil
4 teaspoons Roquefort, or any kind of blue cheese
6 walnuts or pecans meats, crushed
Fresh parsley, chopped

Wash and dry Belgian or curly endive, or both, discarding outer leaves. Cut entire head crosswise in broad pieces and put in an attractive salad bowl. Add chopped apple.

In a small bowl whip Quark, mustard, vinegar, light soy sauce, salt, and pepper 1 minute.

Add olive oil and whip again.

On a small plate, crush Roquefort with a fork and incorporate into salad dressing. Pour dressing on salad and toss well. Garnish with nuts and parsley.

Serve with fresh whole wheat bread.

Seafood

Crevettes grillées au basilic

SHRIMP AND SCALLOPS BROCHETTES WITH FRESH BASIL

4 SERVINGS ❧ 190 CALORIES PER SERVING ❧ PREPARATION TIME: 10 MINUTES

Outdoor grilling is as popular in the French countryside as it is here in the United States. You can either barbecue or broil these skewered shrimp and scallops. Instead of preparing your vegetables on the stove that day, take advantage of the grill to prepare delicious vegetable brochettes: cherry tomatoes, green and yellow bell peppers, sweet white onion, white mushrooms, seasoned with salt and pepper and brushed with olive oil.

1 garlic clove	Salt and pepper to taste
1/4 cup chicken stock or broth	16 large raw shrimp, shelled
2 tablespoons dry white wine	8 large sea scallops
2 teaspoons olive oil	4 metal or wood skewers
1/2 cup fresh basil leaves	

Light a hot fire in a charcoal grill or preheat broiler to 375°.

In a blender, combine garlic, chicken broth, wine, olive oil, basil, salt, and pepper. Puree until smooth.

Pour basil sauce in a medium bowl. Add shrimps and scallops. Let marinate 10 minutes or longer.

Alternate shrimp and scallops on skewers. Brush with remaining sauce.

Grill or broil about 4 minutes on each side, 8 minutes total. Do not overcook.

Remove from grill and serve at once on a bed of basmati rice.

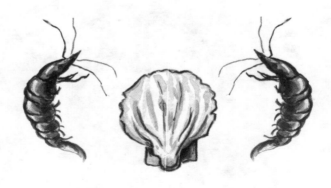

Turbot au miel et aux oranges

HALIBUT WITH HONEY AND ORANGES

4 SERVINGS ∞ 250 CALORIES PER SERVING ∞ PREPARATION TIME: 25 MINUTES

This is one of my favorite fish recipes. The small amount of honey adds a subtle flavor to the sauce and beautifully complements the slight acidity of the orange juice. I retained the use of some butter in this recipe, because the unique taste of this dish depends on it. Have all your ingredients prepared before starting cooking, as it will make the cooking process easier. As with all fish dishes, it is important to serve it promptly.

4 halibut fillets, or any firm white
    fish, 4 ounces each
Salt and pepper to taste
2 tablespoons shallots, minced
1/3 cup fresh orange juice
3 teaspoons honey

1 cup dry or semi-sweet white wine
1/3 cup fish stock or clam juice
4 thin orange slices, peeled
2 tablespoons butter
2 tablespoons nonfat sour cream

Preheat oven to 350°.

Season halibut fillets with salt and pepper.

In a medium pan, sprinkle shallots evenly and arrange seasoned fillets on top of the shallots. In a small bowl, mix orange juice, honey, wine, and fish stock. Pour liquid mixture over the fillets. Bring slowly to a simmer and cook 1 minute.

Transfer fish and sauce to small, buttered, ovenproof baking dish. Cover with foil and bake 10 to 15 minutes, until fish flakes easily with a fork.

Pre-heat a serving dish by holding it under hot water 1 minute, then dry with a towel. Place fish in warmed serving dish. Surround with orange slices; cover with foil, and keep warm.

Transfer liquid to small sauce pan. Over high heat, reduce sauce to 1 cup. It will be slightly thickened. Reduce heat. Beat in butter, bit by bit.

Whisk sour cream and add to sauce. Taste sauce, and add salt and pepper if necessary. Pour sauce over plated fish and serve.

Serve with rice, pasta, or boiled red potatoes.

Rouleaux de soles au laurier

ROLLED SOLE FILLETS WITH LAUREL LEAVES

6 SERVINGS ~~~ 164 CALORIES PER SERVING ~~~ PREPARATION TIME: 20 MINUTES

Here is another quick and easy recipe. I prefer petrale sole, but you can use any other fish fillets. Be sure to remove all the bones before preparing the fish. If you think your children don't like fish, try this recipe, omitting the Cayenne pepper. Ask for their help to roll and attach the bay leaves to the fish. It's fun!

STUFFING:
1 garlic clove
1 shallot
5 ounces lox cut into strips
4 ounces shrimp meat
1 egg white
1 slice white bread soaked in milk
   and drained
1 tablespoon nonfat sour cream
Salt and pepper to taste
1 small pinch of ground Cayenne
   pepper, optional

1 teaspoon olive oil
6 sole fillets, 3 ounces each
12 bay leaves
Toothpicks

Preheat broiler.

Prepare the stuffing: in a food processor or by hand, coarsely grind garlic, shallot, and lox.

Add shrimp meat, egg white, bread, sour cream, salt, pepper, and Cayenne pepper. Mix thoroughly and set aside in refrigerator.

Flatten fish to 1/4 inch with the smooth side of a meat pounder. Sprinkle with salt and pepper.

Spread salmon stuffing on fillets, roll them, and place 1 bay leaf on each side, maintaining the shape by piercing rolls transversely with 2 toothpicks.

Spray olive oil on a grill pan and broil rolled fish 3 to 4 minutes on each side.

Serve with a "Mediterranean vegetable stew"* or "Tomatoes with garlic"* and Basmati rice, followed by a green salad and "Chocolate mousse"*.

Saumon au citron

SALMON WITH LEMON AND CORIANDER

4 SERVINGS ∿ 175 CALORIES PER SERVING ∿ PREPARATION TIME: 10 MINUTES

This is a great recipe if you are late from work and don't have time or energy to cook but still want to enjoy a good dinner. I bake one or two extra pieces of salmon while preparing this dish because I find this recipe delicious when cold. It can be served as an appetizer with a "Mayonnaise with tarragon and lemon"* two or three days later.

A good menu with this is tomatoes and potato salad as a starter. Accompany the entree with fresh or frozen peas. Fruit salad with Kirsch makes a great dessert.

1/4 cup fresh lemon juice
3/4 cup clam juice or fish stock
2 teaspoons ground coriander
Salt and pepper to taste
1 pound salmon fillet, boned and
    skinned

6 sprigs assorted fresh herbs, (parsley,
    basil, tarragon), finely chopped, or
    1 teaspoon of the same dried herbs,
    mixed
1 teaspoon garlic, finely chopped
2 tablespoons olive oil

Preheat oven to 375°.

Coat the bottom of a flat, oven proof glass dish with 1/8 cup lemon juice and 1/2 cup clam juice. Sprinkle with half the coriander, salt, and pepper.

Lay fish slices in one even layer in the dish. Pour remaining lemon juice and clam juice over fish and sprinkle with remaining seasonings. Add garlic. Drizzle olive oil over fish.

Let marinate 10 minutes, then turn each piece over and marinate again 10 minutes. Bake 15 minutes or until done.

Serve with green peas.

Saumon en papillote

SALMON BAKED IN FOIL

4 SERVINGS ❧ 180 CALORIES PER SERVING ❧ PREPARATION TIME: 20 MINUTES

Cooking en papillote means cooking food in a package to keep it moist in its own juices, with only a minimal addition of fat. Recipes traditionally call for baking parchment (which can be found in most specialty food stores), but I find foil far easier to handle, and it works just as well. This recipe is easy to do. There is no clean-up, and it is amazingly delicious. The cooking time is the only crucial part of the preparation; it varies according to the thickness of the fish. Check it carefully during cooking.

2 tablespoons unsalted butter
4 carrots, peeled and chopped
1 large onion, chopped
4 celery ribs, chopped
Salt and pepper to taste
1 1/2 cups dry white wine
4 medium salmon steaks,
    1/4 pound each

1 teaspoon olive oil
Aluminum foil

BOUQUET GARNI:
1 fresh thyme sprig or 1/4 teaspoon
    dried thyme
2 parsley sprigs
1 bay leaf

Preheat oven to 425°.

Heat 1 tablespoon of butter in a skillet and sauté carrots, onion, and celery over low heat until soft. Make a bouquet garni of thyme, parsley, and bay leaf tied with a string. If fresh thyme is not available, use dried thyme. Add bouquet garni to the vegetables and season the dish with salt and pepper.

Add wine and simmer, uncovered, over low heat 12 minutes. Remove bouquet garni.

Spray or brush 4 pieces of aluminum foil (large enough to hold the salmon easily) with olive oil. Season fish with salt and pepper. Spread vegetable mixture on foil and arrange fish on top of vegetables. Dot with remaining butter.

Fold carefully into 4 air-tight parcels. Place on baking sheet and bake 15 minutes.

Open one papillote and check if salmon is cooked. When done, it will have a uniform color with no darker areas. Unwrap steaks, discard foil, and serve on heated plates.

Serve with a mixture of wild rice /brown rice and asparagus.

Saumon côte d'azur

SALMON WITH FENNEL AND PASTIS

4 SERVINGS ❧ 192 CALORIES PER SERVING ❧ PREPARATION TIME: 15 MINUTES

Salmon is not a fish found in the Mediterranean sea. However, Pastis, an alcohol flavoring, is a drink from Provence, so in combining the two, I took the liberty of naming this dish Saumon côte d'azur. Côte d'azur is the name for the French Riviera.

The purpose of cooking with wine or spirits is to enhance and refine the flavor of the dish. The whole purpose of flaming is to cook off the alcohol and excess fat of the dish, leaving behind the concentrated flavoring essences. No calories are added except those from the sugar when liqueur is used. If you have never flamed anything before, practice with a very small quantity of brandy until you can comfortably control it. Although easy to do with experience, this sauce preparation is challenging when done for the first time. Don't be intimidated. It's fun and worth the effort.

1 pound salmon fillet, boned and skinned
Salt and pepper to taste
1 tablespoon flour
1 tablespoon olive oil
2 tablespoons nonfat sour cream

1/2 cup fish stock, (or 1/4 cup water, 1/4 cup white wine, and 1 teaspoon sugar)
2 sprigs fresh fennel, chopped, or 1/8 teaspoon dried dill weed
3 tablespoons Pastis

Season fish with salt and pepper and coat with flour.

Heat oil in a skillet. Fry fillet until golden on both sides, about 8 minutes.

Transfer fish to serving plate and cover with foil to keep warm.

Whisk sour cream in a small bowl. Add fish stock, sour cream, fennel, salt, and pepper to skillet. Stir well, then boil rapidly until liquid is reduced and slightly thickened.

Meanwhile, heat Pastis slowly, ignite, and pour while still flaming over sauce. Stir well, cook 1 minute, and pour sauce on fish. Remember: as an option to flames, you may add the cold Pastis directly to the sauce.

Serve immediately with a mixture of wild and white rice or brown rice. Add steamed carrots.

Baluchons de lotte aux herbes et à la vapeur

STEAMED MONK FISH FILLETS WITH HERBS

4 SERVINGS ☙ 160 CALORIES PER SERVING (SAUCE: 24 CALORIES PER TBLS) ☙ PREPARATION TIME: 20 MINUTES

Steaming is becoming increasingly popular in our health-conscious society. It is the best way to preserve the vitamins and minerals of the vegetables. It does not carry away the precious vitamins B and C because there is minimal contact between the cooking liquid and the food. Furthermore, this kind of cooking does not require the addition of fat, so the dish is very light. You can turn any pan with a lid into a steamer if you have a collapsible steamer basket. They are inexpensive and last forever.

1 pound monk fish fillet or any other
    firm flesh white fish
Pepper to taste
8 thin slices prosciutto ham
3 sprigs flat parsley
3 sprigs fresh basil
Toothpicks
1 bunch of large spring onions or
    scallions, cut into long strips

SAUCE:
6 ounces "Farmer's cheese"*
3 ounces fresh, soft goat cheese
1 tablespoon dry white wine
Salt and pepper to taste

Cut fish into 16 identical cubes. Sprinkle with pepper.

Place each piece of fish on half a slice of prosciutto ham. Top with 1 basil leaf and some parsley.

Roll prosciutto around the fish and hold in place with 2 toothpicks.

Arrange onions at the bottom of the steamer. Set fish on them.

Pour 1 1/2 cup water in the pan with the rest of the herbs. Bring to a boil.

Steam fish 5 minutes on low heat.

Meanwhile, prepare sauce: thoroughly mix together the farmer's cheese, goat cheese, and white wine. Add salt and pepper to taste.

Serve the "balluchons ("backpacks" in French) on the bed of cooked onions with the sauce on the side.

Paella

8 SERVINGS ❧ 400 CALORIES PER SERVING ❧ PREPARATION TIME: 35 MINUTES

This is a simplified and lighter version of the traditional Paella. The combination of meat and seafood gives a wonderful flavor to the rice. Prepare it on the weekend when you have time and eat it several hours later or the next day. I usually serve radishes for an appetizer. I finish the meal with a green salad followed by "Normandy sautéed apples"* or "Summer fruits with rum"*.

8 lean breakfast sausages	4 cups chicken broth
8 chicken drum-sticks	2 pinches saffron
2 tablespoons olive oil	1 small dried Cayenne pepper
1 onion, chopped	1 bay leaf
4 cloves garlic, finely chopped	8 large mussels, scrubbed
1 red bell pepper, sliced	8 large prawns, shelled
1 pound cleaned squid, cut into strips	1 cup frozen peas, thawed
2 cups long grain rice (uncooked)	Salt and pepper to taste

In a large non-stick pan, cook sausages until lightly browned 2 minutes on medium high heat.

Add chicken and sauté 3 minutes. Set aside in a bowl.

In the same pan, heat 1 tablespoon of the olive oil. Add onion, garlic, and bell pepper and sauté 3 minutes, stirring constantly. Set aside in bowl with meat.

In the same pan, heat remaining 1 tablespoon olive oil and sauté squid 3 minutes on medium high heat. Add meat and vegetables to pan. Mix well.

Transfer to a 6-quart casserole or paella pan. Add rice and stir well 2 minutes on medium high heat making sure everything is coated with oil and juices.

Pour 4 cups of chicken broth over rice mixture and stir well. Stir in saffron, salt if chicken broth is unsalted, and pepper, Cayenne pepper, and bay leaf.

Top with mussels.

Reduce heat and simmer covered 15 minutes.

Add prawns and peas. Continue cooking an additional 7 minutes. Taste and add salt if necessary.

Serve in a large serving dish, arranging mussels and prawns on top. A full-bodied wine like a Côtes de Provence or a Merlot from California goes well with this delicious dish.

Poultry

Poulet à l'estragon en papillote

CHICKEN TARRAGON IN FOIL

4 SERVINGS ❦ 238 CALORIES PER SERVING ❦ PREPARATION TIME: 15 MINUTES

Cooking en papillote seals in the juices, rendering a delicious sauce. The foil pouch makes for easy clean up, too. You can cook any kind of poultry or fish this way. The main thing is to add lots of your favorite herbs to flavor the meat or fish.

1 tablespoon olive oil
1/2 pound fresh white mushrooms, thinly sliced
4 large shallots, thinly sliced
1/4 cup dry white wine
4 skinless, boneless chicken breasts, about 4 ounces each

Salt and pepper to taste
8 sprigs fresh tarragon or 1 teaspoon dried tarragon
2 tablespoons unsalted butter
Aluminum foil

Preheat oven to 400°.

Line a 9" square baking dish with aluminum foil, leaving about 4" extra on each of two sides.

In a medium sauce pan, heat oil over medium heat. Add mushrooms and shallots and cook 2 minutes. Season with salt and pepper to taste. Add white wine and cook 1 minute.

Spread mushroom mixture on the bottom of dish. Arrange chicken breasts in a single layer on top of mixture. Season chicken with salt and pepper. Place fresh tarragon sprigs on chicken. Dot with butter.

Fold up edges of foil and crimp to seal, using a second sheet of foil if necessary.

Bake 15 minutes or until juices run clear when chicken is pierced with a fork.

Remove chicken from foil. Pour sauce and mushrooms over chicken and serve on heated serving plates.

Serve with "Broccoli and cauliflower mousse"*.

Poulet Basquaise

CHICKEN BASQUAISE

4 SERVINGS ~~ 250 CALORIES PER SERVING ~~ PREPARATION TIME: 20 MINUTES

Poulet Basquaise is a very popular dish in France. It comes from "le pays Basque" region of northern Spain in the Pyrénées mountains, an agricultural area known for its cured ham (jambon de Bayonne), bell peppers, and tomatoes. Restaurants across France offer Poulet Basquaise as a choice for the main dish, followed by a "Crème caramel"* for dessert.

One large fryer, sectioned into breasts, wings, and legs (with thighs attached)
Salt to taste
1 tablespoon olive oil
1 red bell pepper, cut into small strips
1 large onion, thinly sliced
3 garlic cloves, finely chopped

1 cup mild, medium, or hot salsa, depending on your taste
2 bay leaves
2 teaspoons raw sugar
1/2 cup white wine
2 tablespoons nonfat sour cream
1 sprig fresh parsley, finely chopped

Season chicken with salt. Heat oil in Dutch oven over medium heat, add chicken and sauté 3 minutes until chicken is browned. Remove chicken from pan and set aside on serving dish.

Add red bell pepper, onion, and garlic to Dutch oven. Cook on medium high heat 5 minutes or until soft, stirring occasionally.

Stir in salsa, bay leaves, sugar, and wine.

Transfer chicken and juices in dish to Dutch oven and cover tightly. Reduce heat and simmer 45 minutes or until tender.

Whisk sour cream and add to chicken sauce. Increase heat and boil sauce until thickened, stirring occasionally. Discard bay leaves. Add salt to taste.

Transfer chicken to serving dish and pour sauce over the chicken. Garnish with chopped parsley.

Serve with brown rice and a green salad.

Blanc de poulet aux échalotes

CHICKEN BREAST WITH SHALLOTS AND GARLIC

4 SERVINGS ～ 225 CALORIES PER SERVING ～ PREPARATION TIME: 20 MINUTES

This recipe comes from Brittany, a peninsula projecting into the Atlantic ocean and distinct from other French regions because of its Celtic heritage. Until recently, Brittany was France's Far West, isolated from the rest of the country and possessing a unique culture. Having all your ingredients prepared and measured before you start this recipe will make the preparation easier. This dish is delicious with a salad of warm green beans and tomatoes. For dessert, people from Brittany would probably serve "Pears in wine"* or "Apple terrine"*.

4 skinless, boneless chicken breast halves, 4 ounces each
Salt and pepper to taste
1 tablespoon olive oil
3 shallots, finely chopped

2 garlic cloves, finely chopped
1/2 cup dry white wine
1 cup chicken stock or broth
3/4 cup nonfat sour cream

Season chicken with salt and pepper. Heat oil in medium skillet and sauté chicken on medium high heat until lightly browned on both sides, about 3 minutes.

Remove chicken from pan and set aside on serving dish.

Reduce heat to low and add shallots and garlic to same pan. Cook about 2 minutes. Increase heat and add wine and stock, stirring to dissolve the browned pan juices. Boil uncovered until the liquid reduces to about 1/2 cup, about 5 to 10 minutes, stirring occasionally.

Whisk sour cream, then transfer to wine sauce. Stir well. Increase heat and bring to a boil.

Return chicken with any accumulated juices to the skillet. Cover skillet and reduce heat to low. Cook until chicken is done, about 6 minutes.

Season sauce to taste with salt and pepper.

If you need more sauce, add 2 tablespoons stock and cook 1 minute. Return chicken to serving dish and top with sauce.

Serve with boiled potatoes and fresh spinach.

Poulet au cognac

CHICKEN WITH COGNAC

4 SERVINGS ～ 230 CALORIES PER SERVING ～ PREPARATION TIME: 20 MINUTES

This dish will not take long to prepare, and even this extremely light and simplified version of a classic French recipe will give you a true feeling of what French people consider une bonne cuisine. Have ingredients prepared and measured before you start this recipe.

1 fryer, approx. 3 pounds, cut into
   quarters
1 tablespoon olive oil
Salt and pepper to taste
2 medium yellow onions, chopped
1/2 pound fresh white mushrooms,
   sliced

1 1/2 cups chicken stock or broth
2 bay leaves
2 tablespoons Cognac
2 tablespoons nonfat sour cream
2 sprigs parsley, chopped

In heavy 10" casserole, heat oil over medium heat. Brown chicken pieces, beginning with dark meat. Season with salt and pepper. Turn pieces so they brown evenly on all sides, about 3 minutes.

Add onions and mushrooms to the casserole. Sauté 3 minutes on medium high heat, stirring meat and vegetables.

Add chicken stock and bay leaves to chicken and vegetables. Cover tightly with lid and reduce heat to simmer. Cook 40 minutes.

Add Cognac and stir well 2 minutes. (Add stock if you need more liquid. You should have 1" at bottom.)

In a small bowl, whisk sour cream, then stir into chicken preparation. Cover again and cook 5 minutes on moderate heat. The sauce should be thick enough to lightly coat a wooden spoon.

Serve on a warmed serving dish, and garnish with parsley.

Poulet Normand

CHICKEN NORMANDY-STYLE

4 SERVINGS ❦ 370 CALORIES PER SERVING ❦ PREPARATION TIME: 25 MINUTES

Normandy is located in northern France along the English Channel. It is mostly agri-cultural, producing milk, Camembert cheese, and apples. Its most famous spot is the off-shore shrine of Mont-Saint-Michel, where the Allied invasion began, signaling the begin-ning of the end of World War II. This recipe is a light version of a classic dish of Normandy: chicken cooked in sauce flavored with Calvados, the famed apple brandy of the region, and garnished with caramelized apple slices. The recipe may seem challenging at first; but don't be intimidated. It is worth the effort.

GARNISH
1 tablespoon butter
2 Granny Smith apples, sliced
2 tablespoons + 2 teaspoons raw sugar

4 small chicken breast halves, about 4
   ounces each, skinned
Salt and pepper to taste
1 tablespoon olive oil

1 Granny Smith apple, chopped
1 shallot, finely chopped
2 stalks celery, finely chopped
1 teaspoon dried thyme, 1 sprig
   parsley, finely chopped
3 tablespoons Calvados
6 tablespoons chicken stock or broth
3 tablespoons nonfat sour cream
1 tablespoon milk

Prepare garnish: In small skillet, melt 1 tablespoon butter. Add 2 sliced apples and 2 tablespoons raw sugar. Cook over medium heat until sugar begins to caramelize. Set aside.

Season chicken with salt and pepper. Heat olive oil in a large sauté pan over medi-um heat. When oil is hot, add chicken and brown over medium high heat on all sides, about 2 minutes. Add 1 chopped apple, shallot, celery, remaining 2 teaspoons raw sugar, and thyme to pan. Cook 3 minutes over medium heat until soft.

Pour Calvados into a small saucepan and warm slowly. Ignite with a match and pour while still flaming over chicken. Add chicken stock when flames subside.

Cover pan, reduce heat, and simmer 5 minutes. Remove chicken and apples to a serving plate and cover with a lid.

In a small bowl, whisk sour cream and milk together. Transfer mixture to sauté pan. Cook 2 minutes on high heat, stirring to dissolve the browned pan juices, until the sauce thickens and coats the back of a spoon. Taste sauce. Add salt if necessary. Pour sauce over chicken. Spoon garnish over chicken and top with parsley.

Serve with fresh pasta followed by a green salad mixed with sliced tomatoes and cucumbers.

Blancs de dinde au Madère

TURKEY BREAST WITH MADEIRA SAUCE

4 SERVINGS ~ 285 CALORIES PER SERVING ~ PREPARATION TIME: 15 MINUTES

This recipe comes from the south of Gascony, an area in the south-west of France well-known for its orchards and poultry. It is a paradise for those with a sense of history, a love for good food and wine and beautiful countryside not exploited by tourism. Gascony is close to Spain and has many affinities with Spanish culture and food. Many people particularly appreciate the sweet and delicate Madeira wine. This recipe is also good when made with chicken.

1 pound skinless, boneless turkey breast, sliced lengthwise
Salt and pepper to taste
1 tablespoon flour
1 tablespoon olive oil
1 tablespoon water
4 medium fresh white mushrooms, thinly sliced

1/3 cup chicken stock or broth
1/3 cup Madeira wine or any sweet aperitif wine
2 teaspoons raw sugar or 2 teaspoons raisins soaked in 1 teaspoon Madeira wine and 1 teaspoon warm water
2 tablespoons nonfat sour cream

Flatten sliced turkey breast to 1/4 inch with a meat pounder. Season with salt and pepper and sprinkle both sides with flour.

In large sauté pan, heat 1 teaspoon of the oil and 1 tablespoon water. Add mushrooms and cook 5 minutes over moderate heat until tender. Reserve mushrooms.

In the same pan with remaining oil, sauté turkey breast 3 minutes over moderate heat until brown on both sides.

Place turkey on warm serving dish. Cover with a lid and set aside.

Add chicken stock to pan and stir to scrape up browned juices.

Add Madeira wine, sugar or raisins, and sautéed mushrooms. Reduce 3 minutes over high heat.

Whisk sour cream and add to sauce. Stir well. Cook over high heat 3 minutes or until sauce thickens and coats the back of a spoon. Season to taste.

Pour sauce over turkey.

Serve with Basmati rice and green peas.

Bouchées de dinde à la menthe

TURKEY NUGGETS WITH MINT SAUCE

4 SERVINGS ━━ 202 CALORIES PER SERVING ━━ PREPARATION TIME: 15 MINUTES

This recipe, one of the easiest and quickest to prepare, is a favorite with children. You might also use the mint sauce as a dip with raw vegetables. My suggestion is to start with "Carrots with ground cumin"* as an appetizer, then serve the nuggets with a couscous or quinoa dish followed by a green salad and finish with a custard or sherbet.

MINT SAUCE
4 ounces "Farmer's cheese"* or plain
   nonfat yogurt
2 tablespoons whipping cream
1/4 teaspoon olive oil
2 teaspoons maple syrup
4 sprigs of fresh mint leaves finely
   chopped, plus 4 leaves to decorate

2 turkey breasts, 16 ounces in total,
   cut into 2"chunks
Salt and pepper to taste
1 tablespoon olive oil

Prepare sauce: Whisk together farmer's cheese or yogurt and whipping cream for 1 minute. Add olive oil, maple syrup, and mint.

Sprinkle turkey chunks with salt and pepper.

In medium pan, heat oil over medium heat. Sauté turkey about 4 minutes, until lightly browned on all sides. Present turkey nuggets on a warm serving plate. Decorate with a few, freshly chopped mint leaves and serve sauce on the side.

Bon appétit!

Meat

Porc aux pruneaux

PORK TENDERLOIN WITH PRUNES AND GRAND MARNIER

6 SERVINGS ⚬⚬⚬ 220 CALORIES PER SERVING ⚬⚬⚬ PREPARATION TIME: 20 MINUTES

This dish is a perfect example of new French cuisine: work with the freshest ingredients possible and minimal quantities of fat. This savory sauce is low calorie; the fruit gives it a dense texture. This recipe calls for Grand Marnier because it magnifies and refines the flavor of this dish. You can prepare this dish a day before and reheat it slowly over low heat.

6 ounces large pitted prunes, orange
    flavored
2 cups orange flavored black tea
1 tablespoon olive oil
2 large pork tenderloin, or 2 small,
    about 1 1/2 pounds in total
1 medium onion, chopped
1 carrot, chopped

1 celery stalk, chopped
1 cup chicken stock, or chicken broth
2 bay leaves
Salt and pepper to taste
3 tablespoons nonfat sour cream
3 tablespoons orange brandy such as
    Grand Marnier

Soak prunes in warm tea for at least 1 hour.

Heat olive oil in Dutch oven on high heat. Add pork and cook about 2 minutes, until browned on both sides. Remove and set aside.

Add onion, carrot, and celery stalk to Dutch oven and cook over medium high heat, stirring occasionally, until lightly browned, about 5 minutes.

Return pork to Dutch oven. Add chicken stock, soaked prunes, tea, bay leaves, salt, and pepper.

Cover tightly with a lid and cook over low heat 50 minutes.

Transfer pork to a large, oval serving plate and keep warm.

Discard bay leaves. Whisk sour cream and add to sauce, mixing well. Add brandy. Increase heat and boil sauce until reduced by 1/2, about 6 to 8 minutes. Stir sauce occasionally and continue cooking until slightly thick.

Return pork to Dutch oven for 1 minute to reheat.

Transfer pork and sauce to the serving plate.

Serve with Basmati rice. Enjoy!

Côtes de porc en papillotes

PORK CHOPS WITH MUSTARD IN FOIL

4 SERVINGS ❧❧ 260 CALORIES PER SERVING ❧❧ PREPARATION TIME: 5 MINUTES

This recipe comes from Burgundy, where wine is king and local products include creamy cheeses and famous Dijon mustard. This is a great way to eat pork chops, which are so tempting, but push the fat limit (they contain 13 grams of fat, while chicken is only three grams). Cooking pork in foil seals in the juices and keeps the meat moist, tender, and flavorful without adding fat

4 lean, boneless, pork chops (3 ounces each)	4 thin slices Canadian bacon (about 2 1/2 ounces in all)
Pepper to taste	Aluminum foil
2 tablespoons Dijon mustard	
4 sprigs fresh thyme, or 1/2 teaspoon dried thyme leaves	

Preheat oven to 400°.

Set each pork chop on a square of foil large enough to wrap it in. Season pork chops with pepper, then spread one side with the Dijon mustard. Press a sprig of thyme on top of the mustard or sprinkle with dried thyme and top with a slice of Canadian bacon.

Wrap pork chops separately. Set papillotes on baking sheet and bake 20 minutes. Check with a thermometer for doneness. Avoid overcooking as this renders pork chops dry and chewy.

Let the chops sit in wrappings 5 minutes so they become juicy. Transfer meat with or without wrappings to heated serving plates.

Serve with string beans or "Tomatoes with garlic"* and mashed potatoes.

DELICIOUS VARIATIONS:

(1) Season pork chops with salt and pepper. On each pork chop, place first a slice of Gouda cheese, then a slice of bacon, and top with a fresh sage leaf.

Wrap in aluminum foil.

(2) Substitute chicken breasts for pork chops.

Lapin à la moutarde

RABBIT IN MUSTARD SAUCE

4 SERVINGS ❧ 220 CALORIES PER SERVING ❧ PREPARATION TIME: 25 MINUTES

This dish comes from Bourgogne, a historic region of east-central France well known for its Burgundy wines. Dijon, a city famous as a gastronomic center, is still the home of the French mustard trade. Rabbit is popular in France, but not well known in the United States and often difficult to find fresh. A ready-to-cook, cut-up, frozen rabbit can be used for this recipe. Rabbit is a healthy alternative to beef as it is low in calories and has a firm texture. Lapin à la moutarde is by far my favorite way to prepare rabbit. Give it a try, it's wonderful!

1 large rabbit cut into quarters
Pepper to taste
1/2 cup Dijon mustard
1 tablespoon olive oil
1 medium onion, finely chopped
2 garlic cloves, finely chopped
6 medium, fresh white mushrooms,
    cleaned and quartered

1 sprig fresh thyme or 1/4 teaspoon
    dried thyme
1 cup chicken stock or broth
1 bay leaf
2 tablespoons nonfat sour cream
1 tablespoon milk

Season rabbit pieces with pepper. With a spoon, coat them on all sides with mustard.
    Heat olive oil over medium heat in a large, enameled, cast-iron casserole or sauté pan. When oil is hot, add rabbit pieces and brown on both sides about 3 minutes. Add onion, garlic, mushrooms, and thyme. Cook 3 minutes, stirring constantly. Add chicken stock and bay leaf.
    Cover and simmer over low heat 40 minutes.
    Transfer rabbit pieces to hot serving dish and cover with a lid.
    Whisk sour cream with milk and stir into sauce in pan. Add 4 to 6 tablespoons of water if the chicken stock has evaporated. Cook 5 minutes over medium heat. Taste sauce, adding salt and pepper if necessary.
    Discard bay leaf.
    Spoon sauce over rabbit and serve immediately.

Serve with boiled potatoes or fresh pasta and steamed carrots.

Gigot d'agneau aux herbes en papillote

LEG OF LAMB WITH HERBS IN FOIL

8 SERVINGS ~ 190 CALORIES PER SERVING ~ PREPARATION TIME: 10 MINUTES

This dish is one of the easiest recipes of this book to make. Cooking in foil or en papillote allows us to enjoy lamb without feeling guilty, because there is no addition of fat. Furthermore, the meat becomes remarkably moist, tender, and flavorful.

1 1/2 pound leg of lamb, boneless, all fat trimmed
Salt and pepper to taste
1 teaspoon olive oil
1 cup dry white wine
1 teaspoon lemon juice

2 sprigs fresh flat parsley
6 fresh tarragon leaves or 1/4 teaspoon dried tarragon
6 fresh mint leaves
Aluminum foil

Preheat oven to 400°.
Sprinkle lamb with salt and pepper on both sides.
Spray or sprinkle olive oil on shiny side of a large piece of heavy-duty foil.
Place lamb in center and form a papillote by lifting sides of foil around meat. Pour wine and lemon juice over meat. Add herbs.
Thoroughly seal papillote.
Bake 1 hour or more. Check for doneness by inserting a meat thermometer through foil, being careful not to allow any air in the papillote.

Serve very hot on heated serving plates with steamed green beans and flageolet beans, followed by a green salad and a "Chocolate mousse"*. A full-bodied red wine, such as a good Bordeaux, goes well with this dish. A Côte du Rhône or a Bourgogne is also a good choice.

Carré d'agneau au miel et au poivre

RACK OF LAMB WITH HONEY AND PEPPER

4 SERVINGS ∿ 321 CALORIES PER SERVING ∿ PREPARATION TIME : 15 MINUTES

If you want a real feast and are planning to drink red wine with your dinner, try this recipe. It is elegant, easy to prepare, and simply wonderful.

1 teaspoon olive oil
1 rack of lamb, 12 chops
Salt to taste
8 baby carrots
1 celery rib, chopped
1 medium onion, chopped

2 fresh thyme sprigs, or 1/8 teaspoon
  dried thyme leaves
2 tablespoons liquid honey
1 tablespoon middle grind Java
  pepper or 2 teaspoons pepper
1/3 cup hot water

Preheat oven to 350°.

Heat oil in a sauté pan. Add lamb and cook over medium high heat until browned on all sides, about 2 minutes.

Transfer to roasting pan. Season with salt. Arrange carrots, celery, and onion around meat. Add thyme. Bake approximately 25 minutes, using a meat thermometer to gauge doneness. Do not overcook.

Meanwhile, in a small cup, mix honey with pepper.

When lamb is medium rare, brush it with the honey mixture and transfer meat and vegetables to another baking dish. Place under pre-heated broiler 1 minute. Set aside. Keep warm.

Pour hot water into roasting pan, stirring to scrape up all browned juices. Transfer liquid to sauté pan. Reduce liquid by half over high heat.

Cover rack of lamb with this sauce. Serve it surrounded by vegetables.

Serve with boiled potatoes, steamed green beans, and a full-bodied red wine such as a good Bordeaux, a Côtes de Provence, or a Merlot from California.

Boeuf Bourguignon

BEEF BURGUNDY

12 SERVINGS ✦✦ 260 CALORIES PER SERVING ✦✦ PREPARATION TIME: 20 MINUTES

This light version of one of the most famous dishes of French cuisine is a treasure for busy people who want to eat healthy and well. I usually prepare enough for three meals. One is served the day it is cooked. Another is served 3 days later, changing the accompaniment. The rest is frozen, to be reheated later. Prepare it on the weekend since you need 2 1/2 hours for cooking, with little supervision. Enjoy this hearty, tasty, easy to make stew that carries the true spirit of French cuisine.

1 teaspoon olive oil + 1 tablespoon
4 ounces thin-sliced Canadian bacon
1 large onion, chopped
1 clove garlic, finely chopped
3 pounds lean boneless chuck steak,
  cubed
1 tablespoon flour
1 cup full-bodied red wine such as a
  Bordeaux or a Bourgogne

1 1/2 cup beef stock or broth
1/2 teaspoon dried thyme
2 bay leaves
Salt and pepper to taste
1/2 pound mushrooms, sliced
1/2 pound carrots, sliced
1 sprig parsley

Heat 1 teaspoon of olive oil in heavy casserole over medium heat. Add bacon strips and sauté 2 minutes. Add onion and garlic. Cook until tender and browned. Transfer bacon, onion, and garlic to small bowl and set aside.

Add 1 tablespoon olive oil to the casserole and sauté beef over medium high heat, browning well on all sides. Sprinkle flour on meat; stir and cook 1 minute. Add wine and beef stock, then bacon, garlic, and onion from small bowl. Add thyme and bay leaves. Season with salt and pepper. Bring to a simmer, cover, and cook 2 hours, checking liquid from time to time, and adding beef stock if necessary.

Add mushrooms and carrots to stew and simmer 20 minutes to blend flavors. Season to taste. Discard bay leaves. Garnish with parsley.

Serve the stew in a shallow bowl with boiled potatoes around it.

Vegetables

Carottes glacées

GLAZED CARROTS

6 SERVINGS ～ 105 CALORIES PER SERVING ～ PREPARATION TIME: 10 MINUTES

In America, carrots are usually cooked in water. This is unfortunate as their flavor is diluted, and they become bland and often overcooked. This easy method of preparing carrots leaves them with an intense flavor, a sweet taste, and a luminous color. This is my son's favorite vegetable dish. Serve it to your children. Even if they do not like vegetables, this may change their mind!

2 packages baby carrots, 1 pound each	6 tablespoons raw sugar
	Salt and pepper to taste
2 tablespoons olive oil	1 sprig parsley, finely chopped

Steam carrots with 2 cups of water 10 minutes.

Meanwhile, heat oil in heavy-bottomed saucepan over medium heat. Add sugar, salt, pepper, and cooked carrots. Stir well to coat carrots with oil and sugar. Lower heat and simmer, uncovered, 18 minutes. Stir occasionally.

Sprinkle with parsley and serve.

OTHER SUGGESTION:

Use the same method to cook turnips. You will be surprised how delicious they are!

Tian de courgettes

ZUCCHINI GRATIN

6 SERVINGS ✎ 200 CALORIES PER SERVING ✎ PREPARATION TIME: 20 MINUTES

A Tian is a traditional Provençal gratin. It is usually made with vegetables, rice, and eggs. Sometimes cheese is added. This one is the most typical Tian. It is sold at every market in large cooking sheets, cut into rectangular sizes and wrapped in waxed paper. French people love it as an appetizer served in small portions with a tomato salad. You might serve it as a light dinner, increasing the portions. This dish is delicious when followed by a green salad, bread, and a small portion of Brie. For dessert, I suggest a "Apricot mousse"* or a "Caramel cream"*.

1/4 cup short-grain rice
    (1/2 cup cooked)
2 tablespoons olive oil
1 medium size onion, minced
4 garlic cloves, finely chopped
2 pounds zucchini, chopped
4 white mushrooms, chopped
Salt and pepper to taste

3 large eggs
1/2 cup grated Swiss cheese,
    Gruyère preferably
6 fresh parsley sprigs, chopped
1/2 teaspoon fresh thyme leaves or
    1/4 teaspoon dried thyme
2 tablespoons bread crumbs,
    fresh if possible

Preheat oven to 375 °.

Cook rice 20 minutes in salted water.

Lightly spray or brush a 1 1/2 quart gratin dish with olive oil.

Heat 1 tablespoon of the olive oil in a large skillet over medium-low heat. Add onion and garlic. Cook, stirring, about 3 minutes.

Add zucchini, mushrooms, salt, and pepper. Cook 8 minutes, until zucchini is tender but still bright green. Remove from heat and cool 10 minutes.

In medium bowl, whisk eggs until fluffy. Add cheese, parsley, thyme, and cooked rice to eggs. Stir in cooled vegetables. Season to taste.

Pour into gratin dish. Sprinkle bread crumbs and remaining tablespoon of olive oil over top.

Bake 1 hour, until firm and browned on top. This dish keeps very well when tightly wrapped.

Serve at room temperature or warm.

Mousse de brocolis et de choux fleurs

BROCCOLI AND CAULIFLOWER MOUSSE

8 SERVINGS ❧ 35 CALORIES PER SERVING ❧ PREPARATION TIME: 15 MINUTES

Vegetable mousses are delicate and light purees that are a perfect accompaniments for any kind of meat or fish. Vegetable mousses are very easy to do, delightful to look at, and delicious to savor. Leftovers cannot be reheated but are an excellent appetizer served at room temperature with whole wheat bread.

1 pound broccoli, separated into florets	4 egg whites
1 pound cauliflower, separated into florets	Salt and pepper to taste

Steam vegetables 20 minutes or until very tender.
Beat egg whites until stiff, adding a pinch of salt.
Puree steamed vegetables in a food processor. Add salt and pepper.
Quickly fold egg whites into vegetable puree. Do not overbeat.
Taste and adjust salt and pepper. Serve immediately.

ALTERNATIVES:
Celery and onion
Spinach
Carrot
Turnip
Artichoke and green beans
Mixed mushrooms (both white and wild varieties)

Ratatouille

Mediterranean vegetable stew

6 SERVINGS ➤ 120 CALORIES PER SERVING ➤ PREPARATION TIME: 20 MINUTES

Ratatouille is one of the most famous French vegetable dishes and by far my favorite. What a wonderful variety of vegetables! This recipe is a simplified and lighter version of this traditional dish from Provence. The original recipe requires frying all vegetables separately, using 5 cups of olive oil! Serve this warm as a light lunch with a one-egg omelet and a bagel or 2 slices of fresh whole wheat bread. You could also serve it as a cold appetizer for dinner. It keeps very well and tastes even better when reheated.

1 large eggplant unpeeled, diced
Salt
3 tablespoons olive oil
4 garlic cloves, finely chopped
1 medium onion, finely chopped
2 bell peppers, cut in medium pieces
1 pound zucchini, diced
1 pound ripe tomatoes, peeled and
   chopped, or stewed tomatoes
   (14 oz. can)

2 teaspoons fresh herbes de Provence
   (thyme, rosemary, oregano) or
   1 teaspoon dry herbes de Provence
Salt and pepper to taste
1 teaspoon soy sauce
1 teaspoon raw sugar
1 sprig parsley, finely chopped

30 minutes before cooking, sprinkle diced eggplant liberally with salt to tenderize. Set aside.

Heat 1 tablespoon of the oil in a large pan. Add garlic and sauté 1 minute over medium heat.

Add onion and cook 2 minutes, stirring from time to time. Set aside.

Blot eggplant dry with a paper towel. Add 1 tablespoon of the olive oil to pan and cook eggplant 4 minutes, stirring constantly. Set aside.

Pour remaining oil to pan. Add bell peppers and zucchini. Cook 3 minutes.

Add fresh tomatoes or drained stewed tomatoes and the rest of sautéed vegetables. Add herbs, salt, pepper, soy sauce, and sugar. Taste and add salt if necessary.

Cover and cook over low heat 20 minutes.

Uncover and cook over medium heat 10 minutes or until ratatouille acquires a thick consistency.

Try slices of olive bread with this.

Tomates provençales

TOMATOES WITH GARLIC

8 SERVINGS ∾ 82 CALORIES PER SERVING ∾ PREPARATION TIME: 10 MINUTES

Provence is a southern part of France well-known for its fields of lavender and the landscapes that inspired the painter Cézanne. Although this recipe is best when made with vine-ripened summer tomatoes are best, excellent results can be obtained with fresh tomatoes, which are available all year-round. Tomates provençales are delicious warm or cold. They make a great accompaniment to a dish of plain white rice or Basmati rice and are particularly delicious with lamb chops or fish.

8 large plum tomatoes,
  halved crosswise
Salt and pepper to taste
2 tablespoons garlic, finely chopped
2 tablespoons parsley, finely chopped

2 teaspoons fresh Italian herbs
  (rosemary, thyme, oregano), or
  1 teaspoon dried Italian herbs
1/2 cup unseasoned fresh bread
  crumbs
2 tablespoons olive oil

Preheat oven to 400°.
Place tomatoes cut side up in a shallow baking dish.
Sprinkle salt, pepper, garlic, parsley, herbs, and bread crumbs evenly over tomatoes.
Drizzle with olive oil.
Bake 10 to 15 minutes, until the tomatoes are tender but not falling apart.

Serve warm. This makes a wonderful light meal when served with whole wheat bread and wine, followed by dessert. Try the "Chocolate custard".*

Choux de Bruxelles à la dijonnaise

BRUSSEL SPROUTS WITH WINE AND DIJON MUSTARD

8 SERVINGS ◆◆◆ 75 CALORIES PER SERVING ◆◆◆ PREPARATION TIME: 10 MINUTES

The cabbage family is full of fiber, vitamin C, and calcium. This way to prepare Brussels sprouts reveals a new dimension to this very healthy but often boring vegetable. This recipe comes from Burgundy, where housewives use a lot of wine in their particularly elaborate sauces. The original recipe is extremely rich, with plenty of butter and crème fraiche. I found a way to make it light without losing the distinctive flavor.

1 tablespoon olive oil
2 pounds fresh Brussels sprouts, small
    size, washed, outer leaves removed
1/2 cup white wine
1/2 cup chicken stock or broth
2 teaspoons raw sugar

2 tablespoons Dijon mustard
3 tablespoons nonfat sour cream
4 fresh sage leaves finely chopped or
    1/4 teaspoon dried sage leaves
2 tablespoons sliced almonds, toasted

Heat oil in large skillet. Add Brussels sprouts, wine, chicken stock, and sugar.

Cover and cook on medium heat about 20 minutes or until sprouts are tender, stirring from time to time.

Meanwhile, whisk mustard, sour cream, and sage leaves in a separate bowl.

Transfer sauce to skillet. Stir to coat sprouts. Cook 5 minutes over medium heat, until sauce thickens, stirring from time to time.

Meanwhile, toast almonds 2 minutes on high heat in a small, non-stick pan, stirring constantly.

Garnish Brussels sprouts with almonds. They really enhance the flavor.

Serve with broiled, lean pork chops and salad.

Aubergines mozzarella

Eggplant mozzarella

4 SERVINGS ∾ 135 CALORIES PER SERVING ∾ PREPARATION TIME: 20 MINUTES

Eggplants are very popular in southern France and are found in many dishes. Here is another delicious and easy recipe which incorporates cheese and makes a complete meal if you add olive bread, a salad, and yogurt or fruit mousse for dessert. This dish is remarkably light because olive oil is reduced to a minimum. You might want to change the tomato sauce flavor and produce a different dish every time. Try Chinese star anise and fennel. If you cannot find anise stars, substitute anise seeds. Basil and rosemary, thyme and sage, tarragon and parsley are good combinations as well.

2 medium eggplants, sliced about
    1/4" thick
Salt
1 1/2 tablespoons olive oil
2 garlic cloves, finely chopped
1 shallot, finely chopped
1 cup spaghetti sauce or 3 vine
    ripened tomatoes, crushed

1/4 cup white wine
2 teaspoons raw sugar
Salt and pepper to taste
2 teaspoons anise seeds or 1 Chinese
    star anise
2 - 2 ounce balls fresh mozzarella,
    sliced
Aluminum foil

30 minutes before starting, liberally sprinkle both sides of eggplant slices with salt to tenderize. Set aside.

Preheat oven to 400°.

In a medium pan, heat 1 tablespoon oil over medium heat. Add garlic and shallot. Cook 2 minutes. Add spaghetti sauce or fresh tomatoes, wine, sugar, pepper, and anise seeds. Cook over low heat, about 20 minutes (35 minutes if you use fresh tomatoes), stirring occasionally until sauce thickens.

Meanwhile, blot dry eggplant slices with a paper towel. Cover large baking sheet with foil, spray or brush it lightly with oil. Place eggplant slices on baking sheet and lightly spray again with oil. Cook 30 minutes or until soft, turning them once at 15 minutes. Set aside.

Pour a small amount of tomato sauce into a medium baking dish. Layer eggplant slices over tomato sauce and cover with layer of mozzarella. Continue layering sauce, eggplant, and mozzarella, like lasagna, until all are used.

Bake 10 minutes or until cheese is melted. Decorate with the same fresh herbs you used in your tomato sauce. This dish tastes excellent the next day.

Serve with rye bread or pitas. Add a green salad and "Minced cantaloupe with white wine and almonds"* for dessert. Voila! Dinner is ready.

Sauces and salad dressing

Sauce française classique

"CLASSIC" ALL-PURPOSE FRENCH SAUCE

4 SERVINGS ✦ 55 CALORIES PER SERVING + MEAT OR FISH CALORIES ✦ PREPARATION TIME: 15 MINUTES

Here is an opportunity for you to develop your creativity and inventiveness. Below is an example of a Chicken Cognac recipe. The recipe provides the basic guidelines for making a "classic", light French sauce. I have suggested ways to change the ingredients so you can produce a different sauce and a different dish each time. Change the meat, fish, vegetables, herbs, or brandy, and surprise yourself and your friends with your own creativity.

1 tablespoon olive oil
12 small white mushrooms, chopped
1 tablespoon finely chopped parsley
4 skinless chicken breasts,
    6 ounces each

Salt and pepper to taste
1/2 cup veal or chicken stock or broth
3 tablespoons Cognac
2 tablespoons nonfat sour cream

In a large sauté pan, heat oil over medium heat and sauté mushrooms 4 minutes, adding parsley at the last minute. Set aside.

Flatten chicken with a meat pounder. This breaks the fibers and tenderizes the meat. Season with salt and pepper.

Sauté chicken over medium heat approximately 5 minutes, until lightly browned. Set chicken aside on serving dish and cover with lid.

To same pan, add chicken stock. Cook on medium heat until reduced by a third, stirring to dissolve browned pan juices.

Slowly heat brandy, ignite, and pour while flaming over the chicken stock.

Whisk sour cream in a separate bowl and transfer to pan. Stir in. Add salt and pepper to taste.

Add chicken and juices to the sauce, cover with sautéed mushrooms, and cook over medium heat about 2 minutes. Taste and adjust salt and pepper if necessary.

Serve hot with boiled potatoes or Basmatic rice.

ALTERNATIVES:
    Soaked prunes and orange slices, pork tenderloin, parsley, orange brandy
    Sautéed apples, chicken, parsley, apple brandy
    Peaches, chicken or duck, parsley, Port
    Shallots, turkey, tarragon, Cognac.
    Mushrooms, cod or red snapper, fish stock, fennel, Pastis.
    Rhubarb, salmon, fish stock, parsley.

Vinaigrette légère à la framboise

LIGHT RASPBERRY VINAIGRETTE

MAKES 1/2 CUP ∽ 20 CALORIES PER TABLESPOON ∽ PREPARATION TIME: 3 MINUTES

This raspberry vinaigrette is wonderful on a simple salad, artichokes, asparagus, or even more sophisticated salads with feta or goat cheese.

2 tablespoons raspberry vinegar
1/4 cup canola oil
1/4 cup chicken stock or broth

1 teaspoon Dijon mustard
Salt and pepper to taste

Combine ingredients and whisk until mixture is well blended.

Mayonnaise à l'estragon et au citron

MAYONNAISE WITH TARRAGON AND LEMON

3/4 CUP 〜〜 33 CALORIES PER TEASPOON 〜〜 PREPARATION TIME: 5 MINUTES

Home-made mayonnaise is delicious, easy, and quick to make. The flavor of real mayonnaise makes this worth the effort. I serve it with broiled fish when I don't have time to prepare a more sophisticated sauce. It is irreplaceable with steamed crabs or shrimp, incomparable with steamed asparagus. Mayonnaise is not light and should be used sparingly. You will find this recipe so flavorful one or two teaspoons per serving is satisfying.

1 large egg yolk	1/4 cup extra virgin olive oil
1 teaspoon Dijon mustard	2 teaspoons fresh lemon juice
Salt and pepper to taste	1 fresh tarragon sprig, leaves minced
1/2 cup safflower oil	

All ingredients need to be at room temperature. A small, cordless mixer is recommended though not required. A whisk or a regular mixer will do. Half an hour before starting mayonnaise, drop egg yolk into a small bowl. Add mustard, salt, and pepper. Mix well and set aside.

Half an hour later, beat oil drop by drop into egg and mustard preparation until yolk thickens. Add remaining oil little by little.

Add lemon juice and tarragon. Beat again for a few seconds, and voilà, it is ready! Refrigerate until served. This mayonnaise keeps up to a week in a container with an air-tight lid.

Vinaigrette du soleil

SALAD DRESSING OF THE SUN

MAKES 1 CUP ～ 40 CALORIES PER TABLESPOON ～ PREPARATION TIME: 5 MINUTES

Since my youth, my family has called me "la mère salade", first of all because I love salads, but also because of my interest in making the best salad dressing possible. This is a lighter version of my original one, but still remains dense and creamy. It is particularly delicious on salads which include tomatoes and cucumbers. This salad dressing keeps very well in a closed jar in your refrigerator.

2 tablespoons Dijon mustard
2 tablespoons light mayonnaise
1 teaspoon light soy sauce
1/4 teaspoon pepper
1/4 teaspoon dry Italian herbs,
   (thyme, rosemary, oregano)

4 tablespoons chicken stock or
   chicken broth
3 tablespoons wine vinegar
1 tablespoon fresh herbs, chopped:
   parsley, tarragon, or basil
4 tablespoons extra virgin olive oil
Salt to taste

In a small bowl, combine mustard, mayonnaise, soy sauce, pepper, and dried herbs. Whisk until smooth. Add chicken stock, vinegar, and fresh herbs. Whisk in olive oil. Taste sauce and add salt if necessary. One tablespoon or less is enough for one person.

Sauce au yogurt

YOGURT SAUCE

MAKES 1 CUP ❧ 17 CALORIES PER TABLESPOON ❧ PREPARATION TIME: 5 MINUTES

This yogurt sauce is a useful addition to your daily cooking as it is easy and quick to prepare. It is healthy as well as it includes no oil. Use it on potato salad, chicken salad, and egg salad. It is great as a regular salad dressing, too, especially on a green salad with apple slices, goat cheese, and walnuts. I find it a wonderful accompaniment to poached salmon also.

1 whole egg	2 teaspoons fresh dill
1 teaspoon Dijon mustard	Salt and pepper to taste
1/2 garlic clove, finely chopped	1 cup plain low-fat yogurt

Put egg, Dijon mustard, garlic, dill, salt, and pepper in a blender, or use a small bowl and mixer. Whip the ingredients while slowly adding yogurt. It will take approximately 2 minutes to blend.

Coulis de tomates

THICK TOMATO SAUCE

5 CUPS ∽ 6 CALORIES PER TABLESPOON ∽ PREPARATION TIME: 10 MINUTES

A coulis is a vegetable or fruit puree prepared without any thickening agents This sauce is one of the lightest and freshest of all sauces used in the modern French nouvelle cuisine. It is very easy to prepare and has dozens of uses. It is delicious with a vegetable or fish terrine as well as veal, chicken, and fish. It adds an extra flavor to rice and pasta.

2 tablespoons extra virgin olive oil
2 garlic cloves, finely chopped
1 small shallot, finely chopped
2 pounds ripe tomatoes, chopped

1 sprig parsley
1 bay leaf
Salt and pepper to taste
2 teaspoons raw sugar

Heat oil in a pan. Sauté garlic and shallots over medium heat until translucent, approximately 3 minutes. Add tomatoes, parsley, bay leaf, salt, pepper, and sugar. Cover and simmer 20 minutes, stirring occasionally to avoid burning.

Discard bay leaf and parsley. Pass mixture through a colander, pressing what is left through the sieve with a spoon. This keeps well for up to a week in the refrigerator.

Serve warm or cold.

La rouille

MAKES 1 CUP ~~ 20 CALORIES PER SERVING ~~ PREPARATION TIME: 5 MINUTES

La rouille means "rust" in French. It is a spicy, red sauce used generally in bouillabaisse, the famous "Fisherman's soup from Provence"*. Rouille is easy to make and gives this unforgettable soup its true spirit.

1 tablespoon tomato paste or 1 red
    bell pepper, roasted, peeled, seeded,
    and chopped
1 small fresh hot pepper, serrano or
    other small hot chile
    (2 if you love spicy food)

4 garlic cloves
1/4 cup soft white bread crumbs
2 tablespoons fish stock or clam juice
2 tablespoons "Mayonnaise"*
Salt to taste

In food processor or blender, combine tomato paste or bell pepper, hot pepper, garlic, bread crumbs, and fish stock. Beat in "Mayonnaise"* slowly. Taste and add salt if necessary.

ALTERNATE METHOD:

You may also use a mortar and pestle. Pound the chili and garlic. When it becomes a fine purée, slowly add bread crumbs. Using a whisk, incorporate tomato paste, fish stock, and "Mayonnaise"*. Add a touch of salt. Mixture should resemble a fine porridge.

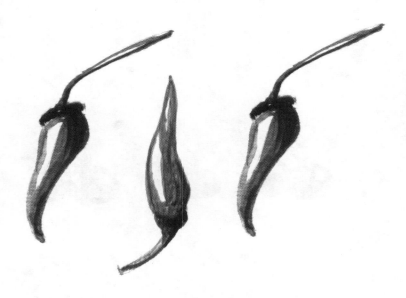

Aioli

Aioli is a sauce with a strong garlic flavor (ail means garlic in French), so flavorful and wonderful that it transforms a simple boiled dish, without meat, into a magnificent feast!

8 garlic cloves
3/4 cup "Mayonnaise"* or
    commercial mayonnaise

Salt to taste

Puree garlic cloves in a food processor or blender. Blend in mayonnaise slowly. Taste and add salt if necessary.

SERVING SUGGESTIONS:

Le grand aioli: Prepare steamed or boiled vegetables: potatoes in their skins; whole carrots, peeled; 1 small cauliflower still crunchy; zucchini, unpeeled, red beets, peeled; leeks, lightly boiled; green beans, blanched; artichokes, boiled. Do not over-cook vegetables. You will also need one boiled egg per person, shelled. You might add boiled fillets of cod or other white fish, but it is not necessary.

Present hot vegetables, hard-boiled eggs, and fish on a warm serving plate. Serve sauce on the side. This strongly flavored dish which can be accompanied by red or rosé Côtes de Provence.

Bon appétit!

Fond blanc de volaille

CHICKEN STOCK

3 QUARTS CHICKEN STOCK ✿ 20 CALORIES PER SERVING (1 CUP) ✿ PREPARATION TIME: 15 MINUTES

A stock is a flavorful liquid made by simmering meat, bones, vegetables, and seasonings in water to extract their flavor. Stocks are clear, fat-free, and flavorful liquids that are the foundation of French cooking, and an indispensable bases for sauces. They are not complicated to make if you have time. They can be stored in your freezer in containers as small as a cup. They must have very close-fitting lids, and it is wise to label them by their contents.

2 1/2 pounds chicken carcasses,
    necks, wings
1 carrot, sliced
1 onion, chopped
1 leek, white part only, chopped
1 stalk celery, chopped

2 cloves garlic
1 teaspoon peppercorns, slightly
    crushed
1 bouquet garni (1 sprig of thyme,
    parsley and 1 bay leaf tied together)

Place chicken bones in a large stockpot or kettle and add cold water to cover. Bring water slowly to a boil, uncovered. Skim foam from surface from time to time.

Add carrot, onion, leek, celery, garlic, peppercorns, and bouquet garni. Regulate heat to maintain a steady boil. Cook 1 hour, removing fat as it rises to the surface. If stock is skimmed carefully it will remain clear.

Strain stock.

Cool and refrigerate or freeze until ready to use.

Fumet de poisson

FISH STOCK

1 QUART FISH STOCK ∾ 5 CALORIES PER SERVING (1 CUP) ∾ PREPARATION TIME: 15 MINUTES

A fish stock is the necessary base for fish soup and for great fish sauces. It is made by gently cooking fish bones, heads, and other trimmings with vegetables in water. The heads, a rich source of gelatin, contribute body and depth of flavor, but if you cannot get them, you can still make a fine stock with just bones. The best fish bones come from fish with sweet, white flesh, such as sole, flounder, sea bass, or cod. When you prepare crab, shrimp, or lobster, freeze the shells and add them to your next fish stock. Avoid bones that are strongly flavored and oily.

I like to prepare fish stock when I can use it right away in my dinner menu. I use the stock to poach halibut steaks, salmon, or any other firm fish about 10 minutes on very low heat. When the fish is cooked, I strain the stock again through a sieve and store in small containers in the freezer.

A delicious way to serve poached fish is to present it warm or cold with "Mayonnaise with tarragon and lemon"*. A salad of potatoes, tomatoes, quartered hard-boiled eggs served with fresh whole wheat bread enhances the dish. Dessert such as "Chocolate custard"*, or a simple "Farmer's cheese"*, and voilà, your dinner is complete!

2 pounds heads and bones from fresh,
  white-fleshed fish preferably sole,
  cod, flounder, or sea bass
1 onion, thinly sliced
Cold water to cover, or
  replace one third of water
  with 1 cup of dry white wine

1 bouquet garni (1 sprig of
  thyme, parsley, and 1 bay leaf
  tied together)
Salt to taste

Rinse fish bones, then place in heavy casserole with the onion. Without adding any fat, cook 5 minutes, covered, over low heat to release juices, turning frequently.

Add cold water to cover and bouquet garni. Bring liquid slowly to a boil, uncovered, and skim the surface until clear. Cook 25 minutes. Salt to taste.

Set aside, covered, until cool.

Strain stock. Refrigerate or freeze.

123

Pace of Provence

Desserts

Coulis de fraises ou de framboises

FRESH STRAWBERRY OR RASPBERRY SAUCE

1 CUP, 2 TABLESPOONS PER SERVING ❧ 20 CALORIES PER SERVING ❧ PREPARATION: 5 MINUTES

Perhaps the best thing of all about the recent changes in French cuisine is that sauces are lighter and healthier. Instead of using butter, cream, and eggs, many recipes now use vegetables or fruit to make a coulis. It can be plain or more sophisticated (using a small amount of alcohol), but it is always full of vitamins, absolutely nonfat, and contains very little sugar. Serve "Strawberry sauce"* with vanilla custard, angel food cake, or baked apples. Try also Peach Melba. Add to a poached peach and place a scoop of vanilla ice cream on top.

8 ounces fresh or frozen raspberries or strawberries

1 tablespoon confectioner's sugar

2 tablespoons freshly squeezed lemon juice

1 tablespoon kirsh (adds 8 calories per serving)

In food processor, blend fruit, sugar, and lemon juice.

Strain to remove seeds.

Transfer to a container. The sauce may be refrigerated for 2 or 3 days. You also can freeze and keep it up to a month.

OTHER SUGGESTION:

Peach and apricot sauce: Replace strawberries with same amount of pitted peaches and add 5 pitted apricots. Follow directions as above. Try it with "Exotic fruit flambée"*.

Crème Anglaise

VANILLA SAUCE

27 TABLESPOONS ❧ 25 CALORIES PER TABLESPOON ❧ PREPARATION TIME: 15 MINUTES

This recipe is a light version of the traditionally very rich Crème Anglaise. This sauce is an essential addition to a variety of desserts. It adds flavor, moisture, and eye appeal to various sweet courses. It is a classic accompaniment to chocolate cakes, ice creams and sorbets, soufflés, mousses, and puddings. Try it with "Normandy sautéed apples flamed with Calvados"*.

This delicate custard requires careful handling to prevent curdling. Using a microwave avoids most of the problems. Sauces have all outside surfaces exposed in a microwave so they cook more evenly. Preparing a Crème Anglaise is a good way to use spare egg yolks. It keeps very well in a container with a close-fitting lid.

4 egg yolks
1/4 cup sugar
1 1/2 cups whole milk

1 vanilla bean or 1 teaspoon vanilla
   extract
Pinch of salt

Whisk egg yolks and sugar in a medium bowl until light and thick.

In medium saucepan, place milk and vanilla bean. Bring to boil over medium heat. Remove vanilla bean from milk. Wash, dry , and save for another time.

Slowly pour hot milk into egg mixture, stirring constantly. (If vanilla extract is used, add it now.) Add salt.

Microwave (medium or 50%) about 4 minutes. Whisk after 1 minute, then again every 30 seconds until mixture thickens slightly and coats the back of a spoon. Do not let it boil. If you do not use a microwave, use a double boiler. Whisk sauce until it thickens slightly. Again, do not overcook.

If you happen to boil sauce, pour it in a bottle and shake it vigorously 2 minutes. The sauce should return to its normal consistency.

Place a sheet of plastic wrap directly on sauce to prevent skin from forming. Cover and refrigerate.

Crème simplette au chocolat

CHOCOLATE CUSTARD

6 SERVINGS ❧ 185 CALORIES PER SERVING ❧ PREPARATION TIME: 20 MINUTES

This chocolate custard is very easy to make. Simplette means unsophisticated in French, but you will find this very tasty if you use a good quality chocolate, such as Belgian dark chocolate. The addition of liqueur adds calories, 8 calories per serving, but also gives a subtle flavor.

2 1/4 cups 2% reduced fat milk
2 tablespoons sugar
4 ounces semi-sweet dark chocolate
1 1/2 tablespoons corn starch
2 teaspoons cold milk

1 egg yolk
1 tablespoon orange (Grand Marnier)
    or coffee liqueur
Mint leaves to decorate

Combine milk, sugar, and chocolate in small saucepan and bring almost to a boil over low heat, stirring constantly to allow chocolate to melt.

Put corn starch in a small cup. Add cold milk and egg yolk. Whisk until corn starch dissolves in liquid.

Stir into chocolate milk mixture and bring to a boil. Cook 2 minutes over low heat, then add liqueur.

Pass mixture through a colander and into a large bowl, using a spoon to press mixture through sieve.

Transfer mixture to 6 custard cups or ramekins and let cool 1 hour. Chill at least 2 hours.

Optional: decorate with a teaspoon of whipped cream and a mint leaf on each cup.

Serve with a glass of white wine and a light cookie.

Poires au vin

PEARS IN WINE

2 SERVINGS ≈≈ 120 CALORIES PER SERVING ≈≈ PREPARATION TIME: 15 MINUTES

4 ounces frozen blueberries, unthawed
4 tablespoons raw sugar
1 cup red wine, Bordeaux or a Côtes de Provence, for example

4 whole cloves
2 large ripe pears with stems left on
Juice of 1 lemon
1 cinnamon stick
1 tablespoon sliced almonds

Crush blueberries well with a fork and mix with sugar, wine, and cloves.

Peel pears and place upright in non-stick skillet. Add lemon juice and cinnamon stick.

Cook uncovered 30 minutes over low heat.

Chill a few hours, basting pears periodically with wine sauce as they cool.

Remove cloves and cinnamon stick. Sprinkle pears with almonds, preferably roasted for a few minutes in a non-stick skillet. Serve at room temperature or cold.

If you double the recipe, cooking 4 pears, keep the same amount of all other ingredients.

Serve with light cookies such as lady fingers.

Terrine de pommes

APPLE TERRINE

2 SERVINGS ❧ 150 CALORIES PER SERVING ❧ PREPARATION TIME: 10 MINUTES

This recipe is so quick and easy I encourage you to try it even if you have never cooked before as you are certain of success. The "Strawberry sauce"* may be prepared several days in advance.

2 large Granny Smith apples, peeled
   and chopped
1 cup of water
1 whole egg

4 tablespoons sugar
2 tablespoons nonfat sour cream
4 oz "Strawberry sauce"*
2 tablespoons Calvados (optional)

Preheat oven to 375°.

Boil chopped apples in a cup of water 5 minutes over medium heat. Drain them. Remove excess water by using a spoon to gently press cooked apples through a sieve.

Combine egg and sugar in medium bowl. Whisk together until fluffy.

Add boiled apples, sour cream, and Calvados. Stir well.

Place mixture in individual, lightly buttered cups. Pour water in a shallow dish to come halfway up sides of cups.

Bake 30 minutes. Chill a few hours.

When chilled, turn cups upside down and set the apple terrine on plates.

Prepare "Strawberry sauce"*.

Serve surrounded by "Strawberry sauce"*.

Pommes normandes flambées au Calvados

NORMANDY SAUTÉED APPLES WITH CALVADOS

4 SERVINGS ❧ 140 CALORIES PER SERVING ❧ PREPARATION TIME: 15 MINUTES

Normandy is located in northern France along the English Channel. Its climate, temperature, and rainfall amount are similar to that of Western Washington. The area is predominantly agricultural and particularly well-known for its apples. This dessert combines two of the famous products of Normandy: apples and the brandy made from them, called Calvados.

Add "Vanilla sauce"* to this dish and you will end up with a quick, superb dessert. Try it if you love apple pie but not the calories!

2 tablespoons butter
4 small apples, any kind except red Delicious, peeled, cored, thinly sliced
2 tablespoons raw sugar or light brown sugar

2 tablespoons Calvados or Apple Jack brandy
2 tablespoons sliced almonds
1/2 teaspoon cinnamon
"Vanilla sauce"*, optional

Heat butter in sauté pan on medium heat. Add apple slices and cook on high heat until lightly browned, stirring from time to time, about 8 minutes. Add sugar and continue cooking an additional 3 minutes.

Pour Calvados into small saucepan and warm slowly. Ignite and pour, still flaming, over apples.

Toast almonds in small, non-stick pan 2 minutes over medium heat.

Add almonds and cinnamon to apples. Continue cooking 1 minute on low heat. Spoon apples into individual bowls and serve warm.

Serving suggestion: top apples with one tablespoon of "Vanilla sauce"* per bowl.

Fruits d'été au rhum en papillotes

SUMMER FRUIT WITH RUM IN FOIL

6 SERVINGS ~ 165 CALORIES PER SERVING (+ 50 CALORIES FOR ICE CREAM) ~ PREPARATION TIME: 10 MINUTES

Cooking en papillote brings out a dish's best flavor. Though parchment paper is traditionally used, I prefer aluminum foil. This dessert recipe is delicious, easy, and quick to prepare, with no clean-up. You can also prepare it in winter, changing the variety of fruit. The rum does not add calories, since it is cooked, but does enhance the flavor of this light dessert. The addition of a small portion of ice cream creates a marvelous sauce.

1 vanilla bean
6 tablespoons granulated sugar
3 bananas, sliced lengthwise
14 ripe apricots, pitted and quartered

8 ounces small ripe strawberries, hulled and washed
3 tablespoons gold rum
Aluminum foil
6 scoops coconut or vanilla ice cream

Preheat oven to 375°.
Split vanilla bean in two and scrape seeds from inside. Mix them with sugar.
Place banana halves, apricots, and strawberries in centers of 6 large pieces of foil (shiny side inside). Fold up edges. Sprinkle fruit with vanilla sugar.
Pour rum over fruits.
Close the papillottes. Make them look like big candies.
Bake 10 minutes.
Place each papillotte on individual serving plate.
Uncover each top and put a scoop of ice cream in center of each serving.

Serve immediately.

Flambée exotique

EXOTIC FRUIT FLAMBÉE

8 SERVINGS ~ 120 CALORIES PER SERVING ~ PREPARATION TIME: 20 MINUTES

This is another interesting dessert that uses tropical fruit. Some of the fruits are very attractive and colorful but not eaten very often. The rum enhances the flavor of the fruits without adding alcohol or calories because it is flamed. It will be a delicious and light dessert following a "Paella"* or "Rack of lamb with honey"*.

2 pounds tropical fruits (pineapple,
   mangos, papayas, kiwis, bananas,
   litchis), peeled, sliced, or chopped
Juice of 3 limes

1 cup each peach and apricot sauces
   (see Strawberry sauce"*)
1/2 cup brown sugar
1/2 cup dark rum

Slice fruits.

Place all fruit in a large serving dish. Add lime juice.

Sprinkle with sugar.

Heat peach and apricot sauces slowly for 5 minutes. Remove from heat and spoon over fruit.

Heat rum to boiling. Pour over fruit mixture.

Top with the hot sauce and savor!

Emincé de melon au muscat et aux amandes

MINCED CANTALOUPE WITH WHITE WINE AND ALMONDS

8 SERVINGS ◆◆◆ 120 CALORIES PER SERVING ◆◆◆ PREPARATION TIME: 20 MINUTES

This recipe comes from Provence, a region well known for its wonderful summer fruit, particularly le melon de cavaillon, a type of cantaloupe. The original recipe calls for a Muscat wine, but a good Riesling can be substituted. Try this dessert on a warm summer evening served with light cookies and the type of wine you used for cooking.

1 large ripe cantaloupe, peeled and
finely sliced
1/4 cup white Muscat wine
2 tablespoons honey

2 tablespoons lime juice
1 tablespoon raisins
1 tablespoon sliced almonds, toasted
4 mint leaves to decorate

Place melon slices in medium bowl.
In small bowl, combine wine, honey, and lime juice. Pour mixture over sliced cantaloupe. Add raisins and mix lightly. Refrigerate 3 hours.
In small non-stick pan, toast almonds 2 minutes over medium heat.
Spoon melons into individual serving bowls. Top with toasted almonds.

Decorate each bowl with a mint leaf.

Gratin de fruits au sabayon de kirsch

BAKED FRUIT WITH ZABAGLIONE

6 SERVINGS ~ 190 CALORIES PER SERVING ~ PREPARATION TIME: 30 MINUTES

The French sauce sabayon is named after the Italian zabaglione, originally made with Marsala wine. This sauce has a crème Anglaise flavor. It is delicious cold, served over berries and sprinkled with toasted almonds. It can also be heated to top fruit as shown in this recipe.

1 orange, peeled and sectioned
1 pear, peeled and sliced
2 kiwis, peeled and sliced
1 mango, peeled and sliced
1 banana, peeled and sliced
12 litchis, fresh or canned
1/2 pineapple, peeled and sliced
Juice of 1 lemon

SABAYON
3 eggs yolks
1/4 cup plus 1 tablespoon sugar
4 tablespoons heavy whipping cream
2 tablespoons kirsh

Preheat broiler to 425°.

Peel orange as you would peel an apple. Remove membrane around the fruit. Section orange, making sure it is free of all membranes by holding a paring knife under the membrane of each section and removing the shiny individual sections.

Place all sliced fruit on individual oven-proof serving plates. Arrange artfully according to shapes and colors. Top with lemon juice.

Prepare the Sabayon: Place egg yolks and sugar in a mixing bowl and set bowl over saucepan of gently simmering water. You can also use a double boiler. Using an electric hand mixer or whisk, beat yolks and sugar until foamy, pale yellow, and warm to the touch, about 5 minutes. Progressively beat whipping cream and kirsh into egg mixture.

Blot dry sliced fruit with a paper towel. Pour sabayon on top.

Broil 3 minutes or until slightly browned.

Serve immediately with Madeleine cookies.

Bavarois aux fraises

STRAWBERRY MOLDED MOUSSE

6 SERVINGS ❧❧ 120 CALORIES PER SERVING ❧❧ PREPARATION TIME: 25 MINUTES

A bavarois is a well known and very rich French custard made with gelatin and whipping cream. It can be made with peaches, pears, cherries, or strawberries. This is a light version of the traditional bavarois. The cream is replaced by nonfat sour cream and egg whites. The result is an amazingly delicate but firm mousse that you can savor without guilt. You might even add your favorite light cookie and a glass of Champagne!

1 envelope + 1 teaspoon unflavored
  gelatin
1/3 cup cold water
2 pints strawberries (2 cups purée)
1/2 cup sugar

3 tablespoons fresh lemon juice
1 cup nonfat sour cream
3 egg whites
"Strawberry sauce"*, optional

In a small pan, sprinkle gelatin over cold water without stirring. Set aside 10 minutes.

Purée strawberries in food processor and strain through a sieve into a bowl. Stir 1/4 cup sugar into purée. Add lemon juice and stir until sugar dissolves completely.

Heat gelatin 2 minutes over low heat until gelatin dissolves completely. Whisk gelatin into purée.

Put in the freezer until it sets on the sides, about 1 hour.

Beat in the nonfat sour cream.

Beat 3 eggs until stiff and glossy, adding the remaining 1/4 cup sugar. Scoop the beaten egg whites on the top of the purée and fold in rapidly.

Refrigerate for at least 2 hours. Unmold before serving. To do so, dip the mold into hot water for 1 minute, and set on plate.

This dessert can be made one day in advance.

Serve this surrounded by fresh strawberries or pour "Strawberry sauce" around the mousse. Serve the remaining sauce in a pitcher.*

Mousse aux abricots

APRICOT MOUSSE

4 SERVINGS ❧ 104 CALORIES PER SERVING ❧ PREPARATION TIME: 20 MINUTES

This refreshing summer dessert is light and very easy to prepare. Apricots can be replaced with ripe nectarines. Dried linden leaves and flowers, tilleul, are very popular in France. They are used as an evening herb tea and recommended for people who want to relax before going to sleep. In America, you can find linden leaves in health food and herb stores. Fresh mint is an excellent substitute.

8 ounces very ripe apricots
2 tablespoons raw sugar
6 dried linden leaves (if available), or
   fresh mint leaves

10 ounces nonfat plain yogurt
2 egg whites
1 tablespoon sliced almonds, toasted

In a medium non-stick pan, cook whole apricots with sugar and linden or mint leaves over low heat 20 minutes.

Drain fruit, reserving juice. Remove apricot pits and leaves.

Puree apricots with a mixer, adding 1 teaspoon of the remaining juice.

Add yogurt to the fruit little by little.

Beat egg whites until stiff, then fold into fruit mixture.

In small non-stick pan, toast almonds 2 minutes over medium heat.

Spoon mousse into individual serving bowls. Garnish with almonds.

Serve with light cookies.

Mousse légère au chocolat

LIGHT CHOCOLATE MOUSSE

8 SERVINGS ～ 130 CALORIES PER SERVING ～ PREPARATION TIME: 20 MINUTES

4 1/2 ounces semi-sweet dark chocolate, Belgian chocolate if available
1/4 cup sugar
1 tablespoon cocoa powder
3 tablespoons fresh strong coffee

1 tablespoon Grand Marnier
8 egg whites
1/8 teaspoon cream of tartar and 1
pinch of salt

In double boiler over simmering water, combine chocolate, sugar, cocoa powder, and coffee.

Alternate method: Melt chocolate in a water bath (bain marie). Heat 1 inch of water in 10 inch skillet until water simmers. Turn down heat and set pan with chocolate mixture in water in skillet

Cook, stirring constantly, until chocolate is melted and mixture is smooth, about 5 to 10 minutes. Remove chocolate sauce from heat. Stir in Grand Marnier.

In a large bowl, beat egg whites with cream of tartar and pinch of salt until stiff.

Mix about 1/4 of the egg whites thoroughly into the chocolate sauce to lighten it. Add remaining egg whites to lightened chocolate and fold in carefully until no trace of white remains.

Pour mousse into 8 small bowls.

Refrigerate at least 2 hours before serving.

This mousse is best served fresh as it does not keep well.

Clafoutis aux raisins

GRAPE PUDDING

6 SERVINGS ~~ 180 CALORIES PER SERVING ~~ PREPARATION TIME: 10 MINUTES

This recipe comes from Limousin, a historic province of central France, well known for its Aubusson tapestries and porcelains from Limoges. This recipe is very quick and easy to make. As well as grapes, you can use apples, peaches, plums, or apricots, according to your fancy. Also try the cherry clafoutis. It is another traditional dessert. Use four cups of cherries in place of grapes. The French leave the pits in, saying they add flavor to the clafoutis.

1 teaspoon unsalted butter	1/3 cup all-purpose flour, sifted
4 cups seedless green or black grapes	1 tablespoon rum
2 large eggs, lightly beaten	1 cup whole milk
1/8 teaspoon salt	1 tablespoon confectioner's sugar
1/4 cup sugar	

Preheat oven to 350°.

Lightly butter a 9 x 12 x 11/2" pretty baking dish. Fill dish with grapes.

In large bowl, combine eggs, salt, sugar, and flour. Whisk until flour is well incorporated. Add rum and milk. Whisk until batter is smooth.

Pour batter over grapes.

Bake pudding 30 to 40 minutes (depending on fruit used), until it is puffed and golden.

Cool slightly and sprinkle with confectioner's sugar.

Serve warm directly from the baking dish. Enjoy !

Crème caramel

CARAMEL CREAM

6 SERVINGS ~~~ 185 CALORIES PER SERVING ~~~ PREPARATION TIME: 20 MINUTES

This dessert is the most traditional one in France. This particular recipe is light and very easy to make. It is best prepared one day in advance. Vanilla beans are expensive but can be rinsed and dried after cooking and reused. Do you know how to make vanilla sugar? Place one vanilla bean cut lengthwise in a jar of sugar and let it stand for two weeks. The sugar will retain a beautiful fragrance. Sprinkle your fruit salads with it.

CARAMEL:
1/2 cup sugar
5 tablespoons water

2 1/2 cups 2% milk
1 vanilla bean or
   1 teaspoon vanilla extract
2 eggs
2 egg whites
1/3 cup sugar

Preheat oven to 375°.

To make caramel, put sugar and water into a small, heavy saucepan and heat gently until sugar has dissolved. Increase heat and boil until light golden brown. Don't overcook, it will taste bitter.

Remove from heat and carefully pour caramel into 6 ramekins or a large mold of metal or porcelain, turning dishes to coat side and bottom with caramel. Be careful not to burn yourself! Let cool.

Whisk together eggs, egg whites, and sugar in a large bowl.

Heat milk and vanilla bean in small saucepan almost to a boil. Remove vanilla bean from milk.

Stir milk into egg mixture. Add vanilla extract if you did not use vanilla bean.

Strain mixture into ramekins or large crème caramel mold. Pour water into roasting pan to come halfway up sides of ramekins or mold and bake 30 minutes for ramekins or 40 minutes for a mold.

Remove from pan, cool, and refrigerate.

Serve in the ramekins. If you use a large mold, dip it into hot water 1 minute and turn out onto serving plate.

Fromage blanc Normand

FARMER CHEESE FROM NORMANDY

4 SERVINGS ❧ 63 CALORIES PER SERVING ❧ PREPARATION TIME: 3 MINUTES

Normandy is well known for its dairy products, especially cheese. Dozens of varieties of Fromages blancs are extremely popular in France. Unfortunately, they are not easily found in the U.S. This recipe offers you a good way to make your own fromage blanc, a light one, and appreciate its wonderful texture. It will be a great addition to your meals.

Quark is a German spreadable cheese found in most grocery and health food stores in the dairy section, generally close to the sour cream and whipping cream. Use fromage blanc as you use yogurt; with fruit, applesauce, hazelnut syrup, brown sugar, or honey. Fromage blanc can be served as a dip by adding vinegar, salt, pepper, and fresh herbs, such as chopped tarragon and parsley. Try it on baked potatoes; it is light and very tasty.

8 ounces nonfat spreadable cheese, 1 nonfat plain yogurt, 8 ounces
    such as Quark

Blend ingredients for 1 minute with mixer until smooth. Fromage blanc keeps well for 2 weeks.

OTHER SUGGESTION—STRAWBERRY DELIGHT:

Purée 1 1/2 cup strawberries, fresh or frozen, in food processor or food mill. You can also use raspberries or peaches. Combine together 1 1/2 cups fromage blanc, 1/4 cup whipping cream, and 3 tablespoons sugar. Stir into fruit puree. Chill before serving.

Serve in individual serving bowls with light cookies.